SISTERS
AT THE WELL

First-century Judean terra-cotta amphora, used to store and
transport wine, olive oil, and fresh water

SISTERS
at the Well

Women and the Life and Teachings of Jesus

JENI BROBERG HOLZAPFEL
RICHARD NEITZEL HOLZAPFEL

BOOKCRAFT
Salt Lake City, Utah

Library of Congress Catalog Card Number: 93-72417

ISBN 0-88494-896-X

5th Printing, 1999

Printed in the United States of America

For our mothers,
Susannah and Arleen,

and our sisters,
Talee, Deila, Frankie, and Linda

Contents

Acknowledgments

---

*W*e thank Diane Orton and Russell Orton, our publishers; and the staff at Bookcraft, Inc., for their efforts in making this work better, especially Cory Maxwell, Jana Erickson, Garry Garff, Carolyn Olsen, and Cinda Morgan. Several individuals read our manuscript before publication and gave beneficial suggestions: Greg Christofferson, Dan Hogan, Joseph Fielding McConkie, Talee Meacham, Dana Roper, David Seely, Susan Shupe, and David Trottier. We also thank Veneese Nelson for her help in checking sources. Finally, we express gratitude to R. Q. Shupe and L.D. Von Speierman for allowing first-century artifacts from their private collections to be photographed, to Andy Ciecke for photographing those artifacts for inclusion in the book, to Carl Glassford for the illustrations that appear herein, and to Joyce Nolte for the pastel that is included in the final chapter.

Introduction

$\mathcal{W}$omen not only constitute an important body of faithful disciples in the four Gospels, but they also were among the first Gentiles to become followers of Jesus, and a woman was the first to see the risen Christ. This work explores the women mentioned in the four Gospels and their relationship to the historical setting of the Greco-Roman and Jewish worlds of the first century. The stories of these women portray the liberating power of Jesus' presence and message as he expanded their horizons and called them forward to discipleship.

The purpose of this work is not to replace the substantial literature that exists on the status of women in ancient Greco-Roman and Jewish societies, nor is it to achieve some sort of synthesis. It is to discuss women in the context of the life and teachings of Jesus.

In preparing to write this book, we have reviewed the relevant contributions of historians—both ancient and modern—and of biblical scholars, all far more versed than we are. Filtered through the eyes of faith and the Restoration, our debt to and dependence on these materials are significant. For the reader who wants more detailed information, we have included a bibliography of the many sources we have consulted.

Performing a valid study of women in the ancient world is challenging, for they are invisible in most historical sources. Ninety-nine percent of what we know about Greco-Roman and Jewish women comes from men. Ancient sources must be approached with great caution in order to extract reliable information about women's experiences. In the absence of sources from women themselves, Greco-Roman and Jewish women's thoughts might simply be beyond our ability to recover.

Cultural diversity during the first century also makes the reconstruction of women's history difficult. Furthermore, while geographic and ethnic variety in the huge Roman Empire account for some differences among women, economic status figured even more prominently in shaping the conditions and choices a woman encountered in her work, family, social relations, and religious life. Economic conditions affected, for example, the amount of time required to provide necessities such as food, clothing, and shelter.

Generally, the status of women in antiquity was anything but ideal. This book takes what is generally agreed upon as their position in the Greco-Roman and Jewish worlds during Jesus' time as the background against which to understand certain stories and events found in the four New Testament Gospels. Our effort is to ask new questions of old and familiar sources. We hope that by reexamining these stories and incidents, we will view them in a new light.

We acknowledge that two of the most important questions that Jesus presented in the New Testament are "Whom seekest thou?" and "Lovest thou me?"[1] These questions, of course, equally apply to men and women. The proclamation of the good news about Jesus' atoning mission is the purpose for the Gospels' existence. Everything else—and we believe it deeply—is secondary at best to the events at Gethsemane, Golgotha, and the Garden Tomb. Inevitably, the focus of all the incidents and stories found in these writings is Jesus and the gospel, or the "good news," he proclaimed.

All of the incidents mentioned in this book have been used in the past and should continue to be used in the future to discuss basic and important gospel principles, such as faith, repentance, service, missionary work, miracles, and forgiveness.

We have read the Gospels many times, but we have not always been conscious of our personal bias. Each of us will raise questions; women will, however, have unique questions and insights into the Gospel stories: the experiences of being a woman, her relationship to family and society, the nature of her daily work and life, and her individual spirituality provide another window through which we may see these stories afresh.

Our discoveries of and insights into the four Gospel narratives will largely be determined by the questions we bring to them. For the purpose of this work, we ask of each story, What does this incident tell us about Jesus' attitude towards women? What does it reveal about their attitude and relationship towards him? And finally, How does this woman or women enrich the story of the good news Jesus and his disciples proclaimed? By no means are we offering the definitive or final word but rather a model of some ways to engage the narratives of the four Gospels.

One of the great surprises in studying the Gospels in this way can be the discovery that the model disciple is often portrayed as a woman. This is especially striking when we remember that the Gospels were written in a male-dominated society. The Hebrew Bible (Old Testament), for example, mentions a total of 1,426 names, of which 1,315 are men. Thus, only 111 women's names appear, about 9 percent of the total. Given such a setting, we might expect that women would remain silent in the background.

In the New Testament, however, we find something strikingly new—women are more visible. The presence of women in the four Gospels is very remarkable, particularly in the passion and resurrection sections—the heart of the Gospels. Re-examining the experiences of women in Jesus' world can lead us to insights that might have previously eluded us.

It is surprising that the Gospel writers often recorded and preserved stories about themselves and their fellow male disciples that reflect their own limited view of Jesus' message. For example, Peter rebukes Jesus after they are told that he would go to Jerusalem and "suffer many things . . . and be killed." "Be it far from thee, Lord," states the devoted Apostle, "this shall not be unto thee."[2]

In spite of their lack of understanding, they succeed in presenting a picture of a Jesus who reached out to women; in so doing, they also give us a picture of the disciples struggling to move from a first-century Jewish understanding of women to a new understanding of women as revealed to them by Jesus' words and, more important, by his actions. Their devotion to the true messages and meaning of Jesus' life caused them to forgo polishing their own good image as they told these stories to a new generation of Christian disciples.

We are left with the clear impression that to Jesus the intrinsic value of women is equal to that of men—an idea found nowhere else in the society of his day. This attitude revealed drastic differences between the ways that Jesus and society treated women, and also clearly demonstrated how he expected his male disciples to treat women.

The New Testament testifies of Jesus' sensitivities to individuals. He treated women as valued individuals. It is not so much that he attempted to raise women to the level of men—for he did not appear to view people as being on differing levels—but rather that he saw men and women as persons, responsible individuals with individual needs, individual failings, and individual talents. Jesus gave very little teaching on women as a group because he never treated them as a separate class with clone-like characteristics and tendencies. Similarly, he gave very little teaching for or about males as a distinct group. The four Gospels reveal Jesus' attitudes towards discipleship in general, not his views on the specifics of male or female discipleship.

Jesus preached directly to Jewish Palestinians. In a certain sense, the Gospels belong to them. But we can find application in our own lives from those preachings today in spite of the fact that we are not the original audience. When Jesus addresses men, women can likewise find application of his teachings for themselves. Likewise, men can find in these stories of women principles of worth and merit.

As we spend time with their stories, coming to know and befriend them in the context of the Church that still tells their story, we rejoice that these precious jewels have been preserved. We hope that as we deepen our understanding of these women and learn from them something of their own discipleship, we may learn at least something of what our discipleship should be. We also hope that readers may come to appreciate the unique contribution that the women disciples of Jesus make to our understanding of the four Gospels.

We then will more fully grasp the impact of Jesus' statement about the unnamed woman who anointed his head at Bethany in preparation for his burial: "Verily I say unto you, Wheresoever this gospel shall be preached throughout the whole world, this also that she hath done shall be spoken of for a memorial of her."[3] This statement is not just peripheral to the gospel, but an indispensable part of it. And Jesus wants us to remember it.

Chapter One

Sisters at the Well:
Women Thirsting for Living Water

*T*here is a well in Samaria. Wives, mothers, sisters, and daughters came daily to draw from it a precious resource in a land without abundance: water to drink, to cook with, to refresh themselves and their families, and to give life to their small gardens of cucumbers, leeks, melons, and beans.

Jesus came to this well on a day when the sun was high; it was twelve noon. Being the second day of a long, dusty journey from Jerusalem more than forty miles away, he and his disciples were weary. The well, perhaps one hundred feet deep, offered life to all who drew from it, and Jesus thirsted for its bounty.

For most of us, at the turn of a tap fresh water gushes out, sufficient for bathing or watering the garden and pure enough to drink without first boiling it. Much of this water is lost down the drain. It may be hard to imagine having to carry all that water home at least twice each day as the local villagers did from this well. But, of course, this was no ordinary well.

"Then cometh he to a city of Samaria, which is called Sychar [Shechem in the days of the patriarchs], near to the parcel of ground that Jacob gave to his son Joseph. Now Jacob's well was there. Jesus therefore, being wearied with his journey, sat thus on the well: and it was about the sixth hour [twelve noon]. There cometh a woman of Samaria to draw water."[1]

Few families possessed their own well; thus, most relied on a common well. Daily drawing water from the well was relegated to servants (slaves) or, for poorer families, to the women of the household.[2] The routine work of women in biblical times did not change very much over the years. The duties were constant and demanding. First-century women's lives centered around their homes, and their daily trips to the well were likely among the few times they ventured out of the house. The well provided the social center of the village and a daily meeting place for the women. And so it was for this woman of Samaria.

She would come with a small, unbreakable leather bucket to draw water from the deep well. She would pour the water into a clay water pot, then carry the heavy burden home on her head and pour its contents into a larger clay storage jar. She probably made several trips daily, as her ancestors and others who lived in the area had done for nearly a millennium before.

The communal well of any village was a natural meeting place for people. For example, when Abraham's servant went in search of Isaac's future wife, "he made his camels to kneel down without the city by a well of water at the time of the evening, even the time that women go out to draw water."[3] Rebekah arrived at the well shortly thereafter. Many years later, Isaac's son Jacob "went on his journey, and came into the land of the people of the east. And he looked, and behold a well in the field, and, lo, there were three flocks of sheep lying by it; for out of that well they watered the flocks. . . . Rachel came with her father's sheep: for she kept them."[4] Jacob and Rachel fell in love at that moment. Generations later, Moses "fled from the face of Pharaoh, and dwelt in the land of Midian: and he sat down by a well. Now the priest of Midian had seven daughters: and they came and drew water."[5] Zipporah, one of the daughters, married Moses.

According to tradition, Jacob dug the well from which the Samaritan woman was about to draw when Jesus engaged her in conversation.[6] It is remarkable that the conversation took place at all, for social custom discouraged a man from speaking to a woman in public. The suggestion, "Do not converse much with women," is repeated several times in the Mishnah (a compilation of rabbinical teachings completed in the late second century A.D.) in various ways and was applied even to a man's wife.

Furthermore, a teacher should not spend any time giving instructions to women, and, finally, a Jew was not to address a Samaritan. That such social restrictions were taken seriously is shown by the surprise of the disciples when they found Jesus talk-

ing with—and teaching—a woman, and a Samaritan at that! The woman herself reminded Jesus: "How is it that thou, being a Jew, askest drink of me, which am a woman of Samaria? for the Jews have no dealings with the Samaritans."[7] The parenthetical clause could perhaps more clearly be translated as "Jews, remember, use nothing in common with Samaritans."[8]

Evidently, Jewish regulations at the time prohibited them from using any vessels touched by Samaritans, as such vessels were considered ritually impure. Jesus openly violated this strongly held custom. His disciples, whom he had sent away to buy food, were shocked upon their return to find him thus apparently at the end of a significant teaching experience with a Samaritan woman: "And upon this came his disciples, and marvelled that he talked with the woman: yet no man said, What seekest thou? or, Why talkest thou with her?"[9]

During the disciples' absence, together Jesus and the woman explored different types of wells and water that might quench her thirst with the water that Jesus had offered her. Her mind at first remained on the level of physical wells and buckets, but Jesus had intended something greater. She addressed him, "Sir."[10] The Greek *kyrie* can be translated "Sir" but also means "Lord"; most likely there is a progression from one to the other meaning as the woman uses it with increasing respect throughout her conversation with Jesus.[11]

The woman continued, "*Sir*, thou hast nothing to draw with, and the well is deep: from whence then hast thou that living water? Art thou greater than our father Jacob, which gave us the well, and drank thereof himself, and his children, and his cattle?"[12] Jesus said, "Whosoever drinketh of this water shall thirst again: But whosoever drinketh of the water that I shall give him shall never thirst; but the water that I shall give him shall be in him a well of water springing up into everlasting life."[13] After thousands of trips to that well, the woman surely hoped for freedom from her burden, but perhaps she also began to recognize that this man spoke of something more: "*Sir*, give me this water, that I thirst not, neither come hither to draw."[14]

The conversation between the Samaritan woman and Jesus slowly revealed her thirst for something far greater than the water provided in that particular well. Apparently the Samaritan woman believed that this unusual Jew could give her a spring of living water, an unfailing source of life, even the gift of the Spirit. After Jesus demonstrated that he knew clearly her past and present lifestyle, "the woman saith unto him, *Sir,* I perceive that thou art a prophet."[15] As they continued to talk with one another, she began to ask the stranger more questions, to which Jesus gladly responded.

"Our fathers worshipped in this mountain." She could have pointed with a wave of the hand when she referred to "this mountain," for she and Jesus were actually at the foot of it. She continued, "Ye say, that in Jerusalem is the place where men ought to worship. Jesus saith unto her, Woman, believe me, the hour cometh, when ye shall neither in this mountain [Mount Gerizim], nor yet at Jerusalem, worship the Father. Ye worship ye know not what: we know what we worship: for salvation is of the Jews. But the hour cometh, and now is, when the true worshippers shall worship the Father in spirit and in truth: for the Father seeketh such to worship him. . . . The woman saith unto him, I know that Messias [Messiah] cometh, which is called Christ: when he is come, he will tell us all things. Jesus saith unto her, I that speak unto thee am he."[16]

This is the first recorded instance in John's Gospel that Jesus openly declared to anyone that he was the expected Jewish Messiah. "The woman then left her waterpot, and went her way into the city, and saith to the men, Come, see a man, which told me all things that ever I did: is not this the Christ [the Messiah—the anointed one]?"[17] She was now a witness to the true meaning and promise of Jesus' words of living water. The new knowledge brought by this woman changed the faith of an entire Samaritan village: "Then they went out of the city, and came unto him. . . . And many of the Samaritans of that city believed on him for the saying of the woman, which testified, He told me all that ever I did."[18] Jesus drew from the well of the Spirit, and the woman in turn carried this living water to the village.

Drawing water is a powerful image. We are convinced that, like the Samaritan woman, other women living in Jewish Palestine thirsted for living water to quench their parched souls. They stood at the well, hoping to draw life from the ancient traditions of their people or longing to discover an inner well of divine power and life. They wanted to be wellsprings of a new vision and hope, to use their gifts to change their own lives and the lives of their families, friends, and neighbors.

The tenacious faith of these women in the face of personal trials and persecution was not forgotten by the authors of the four Gospels. These women, like the woman at the well, had to recognize who indeed spoke when Jesus spoke, and consequently had to ask Jesus for living water. They served as models of discipleship that we can emulate to our benefit.

Chapter Two

The Daughters of Pandora and Eve: Women in Greco-Roman and Jewish Society

$\mathcal{T}$o fully appreciate the lives and discipleship of the women written of in the Gospels, we must see them in their historical and social contexts and understand the attitudes and norms of the larger Greco-Roman world and of the Jewish subculture. First-century Greco-Roman attitudes about women originated in ancient Greece—a deep-rooted tradition[1] that clearly mandated that only male citizens of Athens had any rights.

Classical Greece

One of the earliest known Greek poets, Hesiod, tells the story of the creation of the first woman in *Theogony* (ca. 700 B.C.)—a poem dealing with the origin and genealogies of the gods. Because Prometheus had stolen fire from the gods, Zeus decided to punish mankind by sending them Pandora, the first woman. She had every gift—beauty, charm, grace, skill in women's work—but she was a "tempting snare" and a "nagging burden." Before she came to earth, men lived happily, untouched by troubles and disease. Pandora, whom Zeus made "to be an evil for mortal man," was she "from [whom] comes the fair sex; yes, wicked womenfolk are her descendants."[2] *Theogony* became the standard Greek version of divine creation.

Legal protection by a male guardian was the basic feature of a Greek woman's life. She was considered inferior (anatomically, physiologically, and ethically) from conception. Aristotle wrote,

"The female is as it were a deformed male."[3] Women were generally thought of as wild beasts who must be domesticated by marriage.

It was also a cardinal virtue for women to remain quiet in that society. We learn from an Athenian tragic dramatist, Sophocles (496–406 B.C.), of a saying: "'A woman's decency is silence.'"[4] Women's major function was to reproduce citizens if they were free, or servile labor if they were slaves. The much more important job of training the new generations in their duties was entrusted to men.

Parents often exposed—abandoned without food or shelter—their unwanted newborn infants, mostly girls. Exposed children usually died of hunger or cold or both and became the lifeless prey of birds and dogs (unless found by someone—a mixed blessing because the children automatically became slaves subject to terrible humiliation, especially female infants, who often became objects of sexual abuse).

In the Athens of Sophocles, wealthy families could afford to physically segregate and seclude women of the household. Greek wives were required to be totally faithful, whereas husbands might amuse themselves outside the home with others who pleased them. Women were not only excluded from the social and political life of the city but also from the world of reason and, consequently, from that of love, which according to Greek thought found its strongest expression in relationships between men.

This lack of respect for women was frequently accompanied and facilitated by other than heterosexual activity. Male homosexuality was accepted and practiced. A wife's status as companion was further reduced by her husband's preferred sexual relationships with prostitutes, slave boys and girls, and with other adult men. It is ironic that a system of philosophy that maintained the inferiority of females originated in a city named after Athena, the Greek goddess of wisdom.

Hellenistic Period

During the Hellenistic age (323–30 B.C.), profound changes in social and political life, influenced by philosophy and scientific ideas, transformed the world. The legal status of women also changed, even though society's beliefs tended to thwart these advances. We have a surprising wealth of information about Hellenistic women, especially in comparison with the dearth of material on Greek women in earlier periods.[5]

A new, special status for a small minority of women (the political ruling elite and rich upper class) allowed them to expand their participation in education and similar activities. This change for the upper class had little to do with the vast majority of women in Greco-Roman society, however. The relatively small number of women who experienced the benefits of Hellenistic culture must be weighed against the reality of a harsh and difficult life for the majority of women during this period.

The World of Rome

When Rome became the dominant force in the ancient world, its elite women greatly increased their freedom and independence. However, many of the rights that women gained in the Republic (508–272 B.C.) were reserved for the Roman elite, the Roman matron. Even then, the most emancipated Roman matron lived in a state of bondage as compared to the most retiring Roman male.[6] It is clear that Greco-Roman women were exploited in many different ways, some directly as prostitutes and slave-concubines, others less directly.

A Roman matron controlled property, but in most cases only under the direction of a male guardian. Cicero (103–43 B.C.) remarked, "Our ancestors have willed that all women, because of their lack of judgment, should be under the power of guardians."[7] There were three ways to enter into marriage in Roman society— both man and woman could participate in a solemn religious ceremony, the man could buy a woman for wife, or they could live together uninterruptedly in the man's house for one year.

Under the Empire, however, marriage by mutual consent became the primary form, but this left the women without any economic protection. Divorce was easy for the man. During the Republic, a man could divorce a wife for nothing more than her going out with her head uncovered. Roman family law at Jesus' time made the state responsible for policing the fidelity of Roman women (the Roman emperor Augustus wanted less adultery—a criminal offense for women, but not for men).

Extramarital sexual relations dominated much of Greek and Roman society. Demosthenes (ca. 340 B.C.) stated: "Mistresses we keep for the sake of pleasure, concubines for the daily care of our persons, but wives to bear us legitimate children and to be faithful guardians of our households."[8]

Slavery continued to be practiced on a wide scale and gave occasion to cruelty and sexual license. Especially subject were the female slaves of the household. A jealous wife could punish a female slave for sleeping with her husband.[9] Prostitution was recognized as both legal and sociably acceptable. Female slaves were often engaged in the prostitution trade, which brought great profit to their owners. Further, through the influence of the fertility cults of Asia Minor, Syria, and Phoenicia, prostitution became part of the rites of certain pagan temples. As many as one thousand "sacred prostitutes" were found at the temple of Aphrodite at Corinth.

Roman society debased women through its attitudes regarding human sexuality.[10] Young boys were encouraged to lust after the household's female slaves, always available for their pleasure. Women, on the other hand, could be condemned to death for such activities. For variety, male youths also visited prostitutes who were readily available at public baths.

Women were trained to work as actresses and entertainers of all types, often sexually oriented.[11] Artistic representations from the period generally depicted women in the most degrading situations.[12] Even little children were not spared such dehumanizing acts.

There was little real concern regarding incest in Roman society. Daughters and sisters were simply not protected. Men were also free to be somewhat sadistic to female slaves; for example, a slave could be beaten in her bed.

While Roman law fixed the age of marriage as twelve years, archeological evidence suggests occasional brides of ten or eleven. One reason for such earlier marriages can be traced back to Hesiod's desire to find a bride who was still virginal.

Roman law required a father to rear all his male children but only his firstborn female. As a father, he was permitted to kill his daughter for adultery if she had not been emancipated from his power. The wide-scale practice of exposure always claimed more female victims than male. The words of the comic poet Posidippus (ca. 300 B.C.) are surely an exaggeration, but they contain a gem of truth: "A poor man brings up a son, but even a rich man exposes a daughter."[13]

A father's power over his children was unlimited in Roman law. Moreover, the father retained that control even after his death; for example, he could indicate in his will that he wished for any posthumous child to be exposed.

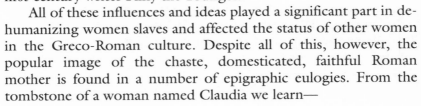

A woman was to not only be faithful to her husband and bare him children but also not survive him. The wife who threw herself into Lake Como with her husband, who was incurably ill, was to be respected, according to first-century writer Pliny the Younger.[14]

All of these influences and ideas played a significant part in de-humanizing women slaves and affected the status of other women in the Greco-Roman culture. Despite all of this, however, the popular image of the chaste, domesticated, faithful Roman mother is found in a number of epigraphic eulogies. From the tombstone of a woman named Claudia we learn—

> Friend, my words are few; stop and read them. This is the ugly tomb of a beautiful woman. Her parents called her Claudia. She loved her husband with all her heart. She gave birth to two sons, one of whom survived, the other died. Her conversation was pleasant and she moved gracefully. She looked after the house and made wool. I have finished; be on your way.[15]

Obviously, we have emphasized the worst in regards to women of these ancient cultures. These ancient societies were both complex and diverse. Many women felt needed, loved, and appreciated. The degree to which a woman experienced life as harsh or less severe varied greatly from culture to culture and from era to era. However, as evidenced by both the positive and nega-tive statements about women from Greco-Roman sources, it would be correct to conclude that quantitatively and qualitatively the negative attitude vastly outweighed the positive.

First-Century Judaism

Jesus lived between Herod's death in 4 B.C. and the end of Pontius Pilate's appointment in Roman Palestine in ca. A.D. 37. Judaism during this period was active and diverse.[16] Perhaps 8 percent of the Roman Empire was Jewish, and most of these eight million Jews lived scattered in the Diaspora (that is, dispersion) throughout the cities of the Greco-Roman world. But the heart and homeland of Judaism was Jewish Palestine. Naturally Greco-Roman influences on Judaism were very strong in the Diaspora, but they were also strong in Jerusalem. We know about several special groups (sects) within Judaism at the time of Jesus' ministry (Essenes, Sadducees, Pharisees, and Zealots). The diversity is not of name alone but also of belief and practice.[17] Besides the division along party lines, those who adopted Greek language and culture differed from those who remained true to Jewish tradition. One of the least-appreciated differences—but nevertheless one of the most significant—was the tension between urban and rural Jewry. This should not be underestimated. The urban-centered survived on the exploitation of the rural poor, who must have struggled to survive each day.

The cities in Jewish Palestine, like the rest of the eastern empire, were economically parasitic on the countryside. Their incomes consisted in the main of the rents drawn by the urban aristocracy from the peasants. The splendors of city life were largely paid for out of these rents, and to this extent the villages were impoverished for the benefits of the city. The ruling elite of Galilee, for example, came in contact with the poor in three capacities—as tax collectors, as policemen, and as landlords. This tension played a significant role in the division of many ancient societies, including Jewish Palestine.

Because Judaism was a way of life, disagreements between different sects within first-century Judaism often concerned religious practice. The five books of Moses, known as the Pentateuch[18] or Torah (translated "teachings" or "instructions," instead of the usual mistranslation, "Law"), contain many directives that govern daily Israelite actions. To better fulfill their desire to always be mindful of God in their daily life, many Jews developed new rituals, broadened the application of many of the laws of the Torah, and in general increasingly detailed how to render a life of service to God.

This movement might have originally been an attempt to transfer the sanctity and holiness of temple worship to areas outside of it, from the priests to the common people and from the temple rituals to daily activities of life. Many sectarian groups within Judaism argued that the purity laws applied outside the temple as well as inside it and that the food on the table at home was to be considered as holy as sacrificial meat on the temple altar. Many groups emphasized the importance of washings and immersions ("baptism"). And the broadened reaches of the population who worshiped God in the synagogues brought a measure of sanctity and communion with God. Thus temple and synagogue became two important institutions within ancient Judaism but caused a stress between which purity laws were to be practiced at home and which at the temple.

We know that in first-century Jewish Palestine, there was substantial disagreement about these religious practices. We have direct evidence that shows that some groups criticized the priests. The Sadducees were prepared to accept loss of national sovereignty so long as they kept control of the temple. The Zealots, on the other hand, were not. The Pharisees criticized both the common people and the Sadducees. The Essenes criticized everybody.[19]

Five important sources from this period help illuminate attitudes about women prevalent within the Jewish subculture in Jewish Palestine: (1) the writings of Joseph ben Mattathias, more commonly known as Flavius Josephus, a first-century Jewish historian;[20] (2) rabbinic writings—the Mishnah, Talmud, and Midrash Rabbah, all compilations dating from the second through the fourth century A.D. but containing older material;[21] (3) the Dead Sea Scrolls, a collection of writings discovered at Qumran;[22] (4) the literature produced during the intertestamental period— between the Old and New Testaments—usually designated as pseudepigrapha and apocrypha;[23] and (5) the Tanak—an acronym for Torah (the five books of Moses), Nebiim (the Prophets), and Ketubim (the Writings)—that is, the Hebrew Bible (Old Testament), including two important ancient translations of the scriptures used at the time of Jesus, the Greek Septuagint and the Aramaic Targums.[24]

Even with these sources, it is difficult to discover the social realities of first-century Jews, especially women, living in Jewish Palestine. In actuality, the vast majority of writings from this period do not give us a detailed picture of what life was like for the common person, regardless of gender.

From what we can glean from these sources, however, we find a society whose central character is the free adult Israelite male. These men own wives, children, land, slaves, livestock, and other possessions. Often these sources reveal a world where the male was considered the norm, and the female, by definition, was an anomaly, a deviation from the norm.

Jewish women were generally excluded from public life and were often forced to cover their heads or faces—or both—when in the presence of men. Some rabbis saw the woman's role as God's punishment of Eve visited perpetually on all generations of women.[25]

Men, not women, were required to attend regular synagogue worship and the feasts at the temple in Jerusalem. Women were restricted from the temple all together during their monthly cycle and to certain areas of the temple at other times. They might have been separated from men in the local synagogues also.[26] The Essene party was much more radical in its prohibitions against women in this regard. For example, the Temple Scroll assumes that no women will dwell in the "New Jerusalem." Wives could reside outside the walls, and couples could occasionally have physical relations in the wives' camp, though the couple would then be impure and neither could enter the city for three days.[27]

Women did not count toward the *minyan*, the minimum number of people necessary for public prayer. Jewish men were expected to pray daily wearing prayer shawls (*talit*) and phylacteries (*tefillin*) and to wear fringes on their garments (*tzitzes*).[28] Women were not only exempt from this daily ritual and from wearing these religious articles but also prohibited from doing so.

Females could not be called upon to read the scriptures in the synagogue on the Sabbath. Many rabbis believed women should not be taught the Torah. In the first century A.D., Rabbi Eliezer said, "If any man gives his daughter a knowledge of the Law [Torah] it is as though he taught her lechery [immorality]."[29]

Men were cautioned about talking too much to women. Jose ben Johanan of Jerusalem said, "Talk not much with womankind. They said this of a man's own wife: how much more of his fellow's wife! Hence the Sages have said: He that talks much with womankind brings evil upon himself and neglects the study of the Law and at the last will inherit Gehenna [hell]."[30] A woman's testimony, except relating directly to a woman's issue, was not admissible evidence in court, according to first-century Jewish historian, Flavius Josephus, "on account of the levity and boldness of their sex."[31]

A Jewish woman, despite social regulations that often excluded her, did have a sense of worth due to the fact that Judaism assigned her rights and powers denied to non-Israelite men. The Jewish woman, unlike the Gentile, was an insider who despite her limitations possessed a defined status within Israelite society.

To be sure, Jews honored the memory of the "mothers of Israel": Sarah, Rachel, and Rebekah. They honored the prophetesses of old, especially Miriam; Deborah, judge of the people; and Huldah under King Josiah.[32] They revered the women who had freed the people of Israel, such as Esther, and martyrs such as the mother of the Maccabees.[33] Yet not even the brilliance of these figures can blind us to this sweeping condemnation by Flavius Josephus: "Saith the Scripture, 'A woman is inferior to her husband in all things.'"[34]

While it is certain that Jewish women often experienced love and respect from their fathers, mothers, brothers, sisters, husbands, sons, and daughters, Jewish traditions restricted their participation in public activity and often tended to demean their self-worth at home and in society. By Jesus' time, it might have already been common for Jewish men to pray three times each day this set prayer: "Blessed are thou . . . who hast not made me a heathen [Gentile], . . . who hast not made me a woman, and . . . who hast not made me a slave."[35] Similarly, the Greeks were thankful they were "born a human being and not a beast, next, a man and not a woman, thirdly, a Greek and not a barbarian."[36] Thus, Jews were thankful for not being Gentiles, and Greeks for not being barbarians—women, however, made both lists.

Chapter Three

A Woman's World:
The Fabric of Everyday Life

*T*hose unfamiliar with Jewish Palestinian society at the beginning of the first century A.D. might not sense the importance of certain cultural details portrayed in the four Gospels. The unwritten part of the Gospels includes that which the authors presume the audience knows, that which they can read between the lines of their story, so to speak, yet which are crucial to its understanding. The Gospel writers likely assumed that their readers were first-century, eastern Mediterranean people who shared their social values and cultural understandings.

A prominent Jewish scholar recently noted, "Much that the Gospel narratives take for granted is surprising to a Jewish reader. . . . Men cared for the bodies of men and the women for the women [in Judaism at death and burial]. Yet the Gospels tell us how women tended the body of Jesus. What am I as a Jew to make of this? It seems to me completely surprising; I wonder if anyone found it so before."[1]

When we read stories about women in the four Gospels, such as the young Mary (the New Testament form of Miriam) betrothed to Joseph, we often find ourselves seeing her as someone who lives in our own time with our own dreams and expectations. The lenses through which we read the New Testament are usually twentieth-century American. The story is therefore filtered through our distinctively modern Western eyes. Very little could be further from the reality of first-century Jewish Palestine.

Despite the growth of several urban centers in Jewish Palestine, the vast majority of Jews in Jesus' time still lived in small towns and villages, some containing no more than one hundred inhabitants. The effects of Hellenism were of course felt even there, but it would have been less pronounced there than in the larger cities of Sepphoris and Jerusalem.

Aramaic had in good part replaced Hebrew in Jewish Palestine as the spoken language of the Jews and remained the common language of the people (though differing dialects existed in these rural areas). Greek was a prominent language of commerce and education in the cities of Jewish Palestine, and certainly it was spoken by educated individuals and members of the upper classes. Although Rome ruled, Latin remained a less-important language of the people of the eastern empire.

Social activities of this period were centered around family and around seasonal religious festivals that faithful Jews participated in regularly. The life of a woman in this world was substantially different than that of a man. Basic to most Jews was their observance of the commandments they received from God at Mount Sinai. God outlined the laws and ordinances that his covenant people were to follow in their daily lives. Perhaps in an attempt to more fully apply those laws to every detail of life, overzealous Jews created extensive amplifications that were passed on orally from generation to generation. By the time Jesus began his ministry, a well-attested text of those oral dictums existed. We know that by the first century A.D., many "plain and precious parts" had been removed from Moses' original text.[2] Even the Pharisees accused the Sadducees of removing material from the Torah regarding the doctrine of resurrection.

When we compare beginning Book of Mormon culture, predating Jesus' ministry by six hundred years, with that of first-century Judaism, we are confronted with what seems to be two separate religions. We find little evidence that the Nephites had knowledge of all the injunctions of first-century Judaism. This might imply that during the exile and before their return to Jewish Palestine, the Jews altered to some extent either their biblical texts or their views of those texts, thus producing a changed Judaism.

A woman's life in Jewish Palestine was shaped by many forces, but fundamental to this world were the writings found in the first-century Torah scrolls and, perhaps more important, the rabbinical interpretations of those writings. These had a great influence upon a woman's daily experience and activity throughout her life.[3]

Birth and Childhood

A female's birth into the world signaled a certain approach to child rearing. This particular way of relating to a daughter characterized her relationship with not only her immediate family but also everyone she came in contact with throughout her life.

According to Mosaic regulation, a woman became ritually impure when she delivered a child. It was a lengthy impurity that was divided into two distinct stages. During stage one—which lasted for one week if the child was a boy, two weeks if a girl—the mother was impure as if she were menstruating; that is, she could not have sexual relations with her spouse. Stage two lasted for thirty-three or sixty-six days, depending on the sex of the child (longer for female infants). During this stage the woman could not touch "anything holy."[4] The period concluded with the presentation of offerings: either a lamb as a burnt offering and a bird (pigeon or dove) as a sin offering, or two birds if she could not afford a lamb.[5]

Unlike parents in pagan culture, the Jews were enjoined to keep all their children (including female infants) alive. Flavius Josephus wrote, "The law, moreover, enjoins us to bring up all our offspring."[6] When first-century Roman historian Tacitus reported that the Jews "regard it as a crime to kill any late-born child [one that was not desired]," it was with disgust.[7] Nevertheless, female infants were not treated the same as their male counterparts, and contemporary celebrations and ritual seem to have reinforced such attitudes.

Child rearing was done entirely by women. Childhood was almost nonexistent for Jewish girls: they were taught domestic roles and duties as soon as they were able. Their tasks were often difficult and physically demanding. From the beginning they were taught that the public world was a male world from which they were mostly excluded.

Since the father took no part in child rearing until the children reached puberty—and then only with sons—relations between fathers and daughters were usually distant (there were exceptions, of course). A father's lifelong worry was that an unruly daughter would shame him and the entire family, especially in a small village environment of Jewish Palestine. He worried that she might fail to get married, would be raped, might be unfaithful when married, or become pregnant before marriage.

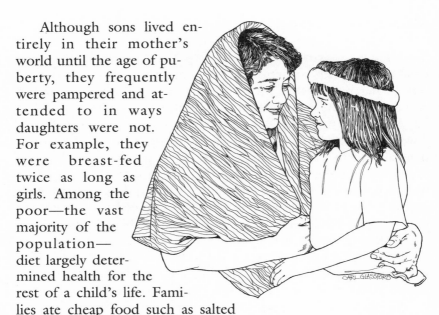

Although sons lived entirely in their mother's world until the age of puberty, they frequently were pampered and attended to in ways daughters were not. For example, they were breast-fed twice as long as girls. Among the poor—the vast majority of the population— diet largely determined health for the rest of a child's life. Families ate cheap food such as salted fish if they were near the Mediterranean Sea or the Sea of Galilee. Their bread was made from low grades of local wheat, low-quality grain imported from Egypt, or barley. They drank beer or wine diluted with water and sweetened their food with honey. They seldom ate meat, mostly reserving it for festival occasions, and had fish on the Sabbath. Date palms were a treat for young children and adults alike. Some evidence exists that the kinds of food and portions available to female children of the family were not equal to that given their male siblings. Daughters always took second place, even when it came to the basic necessities of life.

Becoming a Woman

As they physically matured, young women learned another aspect about themselves and their impact on the family: menstruation resulted in seven days of impurity. Keeping the rules of cleanness meant that while menstruating they could not prepare food to be eaten by others who observed various interpretations of the law of Moses. Also during that week, the female members of the family had to take special care to demarcate the places in which they walked, sat, and stood, since their "uncleanness" extended even to objects upon which they stood, sat, or lay.

Thus, a woman had a large amount of washing to do at the end of the seven days. She was also required to immerse her whole body at the end of the purification period. For those who did not live near a spring or river, a pool called a *miqveh* was cut into bedrock.[8] This reflected the view that purifying water should not be carried in anything that a person built. In rabbinic parlance, it should not be "drawn water."

Numerous types of such pools have been found, all cut into bedrock. They were deep enough (nearly seven feet) for a woman to easily immerse herself by walking down the steps leading to the bottom. The pools were filled with means of channels that carried rain or spring water; they could not be drained. These pools were distinctive—they were not bathtubs, storage cisterns, or recreational swimming pools. Because they were deep and had a relatively large surface area (7 x 10 feet), they held a lot of water (3,800 gallons). The steps took up a major portion of the pool's interior since they went all the way to the bottom. Purification pools were cold and dark; even in a hot climate like Jewish Palestine, a large pool of water in bedrock, covered by a roof, was cold.

A woman descended impure along one side of the stairs and ascended pure along the other side (the difference was marked by a physical division in the steps). The washing of self, articles of clothing, and other items made impure during this period complicated a woman's everyday life as it interrupted normal domestic relations and access to the temple. It also potentially created incredible emotional stress.

A Woman's Private World

The private world of women was the world of the family. Loyalty, obedience, hard work, and sensitivity to family honor were their principal values. This private world—the household—was the domain of women. It was a closed sphere marked off by inviolate boundaries, which commanded absolute loyalty of all members. The woman's responsibility included childbearing, clothing, food distribution, and other tasks needed to run the household.

Women had little or no contact with males outside of their extended family group. Life in Jewish Palestine was organized so that men and women moved in separate circles that might touch but never really overlap.

A certain spiritual significance was accredited to the woman's role in the home, however. Rabbi Jacob said, "He who has no wife dwells without good, without help, without joy, without blessing, and without atonement."[9] The mother's spiritual influence is perhaps indicated by the fact that a child was considered a Jew by the rabbis only if its mother was a Jewess, while the father's religion was of no consequence.

Wedding and Marriage

Marriage was of course one of the most significant stages of a woman's life. Entrance into marriage was celebrated with a lavish wedding feast. The ritual included having the bride brought to the wedding by the groomsman, while the bridegroom was accompanied to the celebration by the bridesmaids. A steward was in charge of the feast and made all the arrangements. To separate this important celebration from other festive occasions, attendees were often required to wear a special wedding garment to gain admission to the feast.

By the marriage contract, the new husband was bound to provide food, clothing, and material needs for his wife, and a woman could demand these things before a court. While generally it was impossible for a woman to sue for divorce, under Jewish law a woman could leave her husband and return to her parents' home, thus precipitating a divorce in most cases.

It was not uncommon for the new bride to be twelve years or younger at the time of marriage.[10] Many females gave birth to several children, many of whom did not survive the first year of life, and then died themselves before reaching middle age. It has been estimated that one in five pregnancies resulted in the death of the mother during this period. One woman living during the first century was married at eleven, gave birth to six children, lost five of them, and died at twenty-seven.[11]

A new wife was sometimes subjected to another humiliating experience—the procedure outlined to determine if the young bride was a virgin.[12] If a husband claimed that his new bride, contrary to her father's protestations, was not a virgin on the day of her marriage, the bride's parents were summoned to produce the stained linen from the marriage bed as proof of defloration. Otherwise the judges would find that the girl had been a prostitute while still living under her father's roof, and she would be stoned to death. The linen of the marriage bed seemed the sole admissible proof of the bride's virginity. The combined emotional and psychological stress for a young girl moving into the adult world must have been incredible. In many cases, a new bride was like a stranger in the house, a sort of long-lost relative never quite integrated into her husband's extended family.

A Woman's World

Women relied heavily on the companionship of other women. This women's world was a female's only domain outside the confines of the household and constituted a virtual subculture within the large society. In many cases the ties between women were stronger than those between husband and wife, and frequently women worked as hard to keep men out of this world as the men did to prevent the entry of women into their world.

Women often closed ranks against males in attempts to protect each other. Depending on the living situation, a woman might see the males in her family at meals and, in the case of a husband, at bedtime. Therefore, social conversation was perhaps the most important communication among women.

The house was linked to the public world—the male world— by all adult males of the family, though especially by the family patriarch. Honorable women never crossed into the public sphere unless they were widows. A widow without a son was allowed to assume male roles to ensure the survival of her family.

Few women in antiquity—this would also be true of Jewish Palestine—could read or write, and therefore it is difficult to find a women's literature of that time. We do not know how they reacted to their religious impurity each month, how they felt on the day they were married, nor what a young mother thought when her first daughter was born.

Women spent most of their time fulfilling their household

duties. They suffered from a poor diet, backbreaking work, and bad health. Our view of Jewish women during Jesus' time, therefore, basically comes from men speaking with varying degrees of sensitivity to the conditions of a woman's life. These sources all agree that women were sanctified through the good deeds of the men in their lives—their fathers, husbands, and sons. Like the earth and time, the fruits of the field and of the herd, women were blessed through the men.

The Four Gospels' View

The four Gospels represent a profound departure from the centuries-old traditions of Jewish Palestinian culture. Jesus' teachings and interactions with women challenged both Jewish and Greco-Roman ideas. In a certain sense, it went further than that— the Messiah of all people fulfilled Mosaic ideology, with its detailed spinoffs, and raised social and doctrinal standards to a new level. Jesus' rejection of certain portions of then socially acceptable Mosaic regulations regarding women confronts us finally with Jesus' unprecedented claim to authority.[13]

All four Gospels, despite their differences, present us with the same picture of Jesus as one who not only showed concern for the well-being of women but also acknowledged their true worth and took note of their ideas and opinions whether he accepted or rejected those ideas.

The stories found in the Gospels demonstrate an equal concern for women and men. Both were in need of forgiveness. Like men, women needed to hear his message of change, and Jesus expected them both to respond to his call. The Gospel writers preserved these stories and presented them to a Greco-Roman world that often found them offensive.

Chapter Four

Separate Witnesses:
The Four Gospels in Perspective

$\mathcal{T}$he New Testament contains four distinct portrayals of Jesus' interaction with women. Despite that, the Gospels of Matthew, Mark, Luke, and John share many crucial components; for example, all four contain lengthy accounts of the women at the foot of the cross and at the tomb on Resurrection morning. This is one reason why students of the New Testament have used Gospel harmonies to study Jesus' ministry as described in the four Gospels. A Gospel harmony, sometimes called a synopsis, endeavors to weave all the details of the Gospel tradition into a single chronological strand or sequence.[1]

A Gospel harmony usually presents the Gospels in parallel columns in such a way that a reader sees all similarities in the texts at a single glance.[2] Any study of Jesus' life should include all relevant texts (in particular, the four Gospels). However, the unwise use of a Gospel harmony—taking the four Gospels as a whole—can distort the historical setting of each story. The process of harmonization has more often taken place among the synoptic Gospels of Matthew, Mark, and Luke, even among earliest scribes and copyists.

It is important to resist the temptation to harmonize these Gospel accounts in order to create one story out of four or to subordinate one Gospel account to the others. The differences are sometimes merely stylistic, though a few may be more significant. Undoubtedly each Gospel writer preserved a separate and distinct account of Jesus' life and ministry for a good reason.

Jesus proclaimed the gospel, or the good news (the English word *gospel* derives from the Anglo-Saxon *godspell*, which means "good tidings").[3] Jesus declared the gospel—i.e., that the kingdom of God had come through him—and the New Testament writers presented the good news about Jesus.[4] The title given to their work from the second century onwards is significant: the Gospel *according to* Matthew, the Gospel *according to* Mark, and so on. So, although Jesus proclaimed a single gospel, each evangelist presented the life of Jesus in accordance with his own perspective and purpose. The four Gospels are not biographies; rather, they are testimonies. Each writer thus gave his particular testimony, and as a result we now have four Gospels.

Gospel Mosaics

Although we have a tendency to want one picture of Jesus' ministry—a single Gospel, as it were—the Gospel narratives do not make a single picture, but four beautiful mosaics. They are the words and actions of Jesus as interpreted by authentic witnesses. We do not need to cut and paste them together to form a single picture. "[The first harmony's] declared purpose," a New Testament scholar wrote, was "to fuse parallel texts into one single text," and to do so, the compiler had to harmonize and diminish the difference or supposed contradiction between the stories.[5]

If we had four mosaics giving different representations of the same scene, it would likely not occur to us to say, "These mosaics are so beautiful that I do not want to lose any of them; I shall demolish them and use the enormous pile of stones to make a single mosaic that combines all four of them." Trying to combine the pieces would be an outrageous affront to the artists and a tragic loss of their works. Because the four Gospels are different from each other, we must study each one for itself, without demolishing it and without using the debris to reconstruct anew the lives of Jesus and his disciples. Even though it is useful to study the Gospels with the aid of such tools as a harmony, we must remember that such tools can, in fact, divert our attention from the real drama and the essential issues raised by each of the Gospels.

Individual Witnesses

The first three Gospels—Matthew, Mark, and Luke—are called the synoptic Gospels because they share similar material. The Greek word *synoptikos* means "to see the whole together, to take a comprehensive view."[6] Even so, each is unique and has much detail that is not shared by the other Gospels. John's work stands apart from the synoptic Gospels because it has a significant amount of unique material, including several important discourses delivered by Jesus that are not recorded anywhere else.[7]

Each of the four Gospels highlights Jesus' interaction with women in different ways. The following brief introduction of each will help set the stage for our further discussions regarding Jesus, women, and the four Gospels.

Mark's Gospel

Perhaps the earliest of the four Gospels, Mark has received the least attention among the Latter-day Saints.[8] It is generally agreed that Mark was responsible for forming the first chronological outline of Jesus' life. In general, it can be safely assumed that Mark, also known as John Mark—a companion of Paul, cousin of Barnabas, and associate of Peter—addressed primarily Gentile Christians, not Jewish Christians, because he had to explain Jewish customs and beliefs to them.[9] For example, in regard to foods, the author made the following digression: "For the Pharisees, and all the Jews, except they wash their hands oft, eat not, holding the traditions of the elders."[10] Mark also had to translate into Greek words and phrases that were originally used in Aramaic—a language closely related to Hebrew and spoken by Jesus. Thus, when Jesus raised up the daughter of Jairus, he said, "Talitha cumi." Mark immediately added, "which is, being interpreted, Damsel, I say unto thee, arise."[11]

To Mark, Jesus was the model disciple, expressing his willingness to do the Father's will as an example of that discipleship. Mark presented other models of discipleship, however, counterparts of Jesus, women followers of Christ. Mark's Gospel has the least amount of unique material, being only about seven percent exclusive. This Gospel contains 661 verses, of which some 80 percent are reproduced in Matthew and about 65 percent in Luke. However, only in Mark do we get an additional insight about Herodias.[12] Mark was also the only one to preserve the identity of one of the female disciples, Salome. She was at the cross and went along with several other women to the tomb with "sweet spices" so that they might anoint the body of Jesus.[13] Mark told us explicitly that all the male disciples of Jesus fled and that women remained at the cross and followed Jesus' body to the tomb.

It is generally assumed that Matthew and Luke made use of Mark's text in writing their Gospels a few years later.

Matthew's Gospel

With a total of 1,068 verses, Matthew's Gospel is significantly longer than Mark's. Matthew added to the record a great deal concerning Jesus' teachings, as well as providing the nativity story totally absent from Mark. Matthew might have had another name, Levi, which is the name given to the tax (toll) collector who followed Jesus.[14]

When Matthew wrote his Gospel, he used several sources to help compose his story.[15] Among them were the Greek Old Testament, the *Septuagint*;[16] a Greek text of Mark's Gospel; and his own personal reminiscences.

The Gospel of Matthew addresses an originally Jewish congregation and is therefore interested in demonstrating Jesus' fulfillment of Jewish scripture. He made references to nearly ninety Old

Testament passages relating to the life of Jesus. Emphasizing Jewish concerns such as Jesus' descent from King David, the fulfillment of biblical prophecies, and the fulfillment and interpretation of the law of Moses, Matthew portrayed Jesus as having limited his earthly mission to Jews.

Following the resurrection, the mission was extended to all. Neither Jew nor Gentile, male or female was privileged; judgment was based not on race, class, gender, or ethnicity, but on doing the will of heaven.

Only Matthew preserved the fact that women were present on two important occasions—the feeding of the five thousand and the four thousand: "And they that had eaten were about five thousand men, beside women and children."[17] And again, "they that did eat were four thousand men, beside women and children."[18]

Among the Gospel's specific strengths, Matthew emphasized the importance of service.[19] In particular, women represented both the ideal of service that Jesus requests of his disciples and the model of fidelity that the Gospel requests of its followers.[20] But this service is not equated with women's stereotypical duty as servants to spouse or children. Rather, women who appear apart from husband, father, or son assume positive, active roles in the Gospel. Matthew clearly recognized the contributions made to the growth of the Church by women disciples.

The central role of women in the final episode of the Gospel should raise the question of women's importance throughout the entire narrative. In Matthew the faithful women found at the cross and the tomb typify a pattern of positive women characters—with the exception of Herodias and her daughter—who either come to Jesus in faith for healing, perform loving service to him, stand as examples of righteousness to be emulated, or speak the truth when another disciple does not. This almost universally positive portrayal stands in striking contrast to the dominantly negative portrait of many of the men Jesus came in contact with during his ministry.[21]

Luke's Gospel

The Gospel of Luke is part of a two-volume work, the Gospel itself and the Acts of the Apostles.[22] Luke himself reminds his audience of this as he begins the Acts of the Apostles with the words: "The former treatise have I made, O Theophilus, of all that Jesus began both to do and teach, until the day in which he was taken up."[23] The "former treatise" is, of course, the Gospel of Luke.[24] Luke apparently edited Mark's Gospel and supplied new information when he wrote his work. Luke has 1,149 verses, significantly longer than Mark's Gospel. Some 59 percent of the material found in Luke's writing is unique to his Gospel.

The Gospel of Luke contains a great deal of material about women that is found in no other Gospel. Luke highlighted women as being among the followers of Jesus, serving as subjects of his teaching and objects of his healings, and living as models of service.

In fact, the number of women depicted in Luke and their significant presence in the narrative are surprising. Here and only here do we find the story of Elisabeth, the mother of John the Baptist and a model of faith; Anna, a prophetess, who appeared in the temple at Jesus' presentation; Joanna and Susanna, traveling companions of Jesus, along with Mary Magdalene; and Mary and Martha, the two sisters who provided Jesus with hospitality and listened to his word.

Although Mary, the mother of Jesus, is mentioned in Mark and Matthew, in Luke she comes to life as a model for believers with the words, "And blessed is she that believed."[25] Mary, as a believing disciple, gradually came to understand the mission of her child.[26] As evidenced from Mary's response to the shepherds' message, Simeon's prophecy, and Jesus' own words in the temple, no one had a complete understanding of the Messiah's mission.[27] Her appearance in the upper room following the resurrection demonstrated that she was among the earliest believers of the resurrection and, like other disciples, understood her son's mission.[28]

In addition to this, women appear in stories and parables found nowhere else. In a great miracle Jesus raised up from the dead the only son of the widow of Nain.[29] We have a long story about the anointing of Jesus' feet by a female sinner in a Pharisee's home.[30] There is also the healing of the woman on the Sabbath.[31] Finally, there are special parables about women: the parable of the lost coin and the parable of the persistent widow and the unjust judge.[32] These parables are paired with similar stories featuring men. This pairing of parables demonstrates an awareness of women in his audience.

John's Gospel

Towards the end of the first century, John, son of Zebedee, resided in Ephesus, where he probably composed this work.[33] One cannot help but notice that the Gospel of John is something unique. In the synoptic Gospels Jesus often speaks in parables and aphorisms (short, pithy sayings, usually with a sharp edge); in John he rarely does. The Gospel of John, unlike the other Gospels, begins not with a story but rather a *song*. John 1:1–18, known traditionally as the Prologue to John, consists of a hymn— a celebration of the coming of the Word of God.

Yet, this hymn also holds the key to the overall structure of the entire Gospel. "He came unto his own, and his own received him not. But as many as received him, to them gave he power to become the sons [*children* in Greek] of God, even to them that believe on his name."[34] These two verses help to explain the break in the narrative that occurs between chapter 12 and chapter 13. Chapters 1–12 narrate Jesus' coming to his own. Jesus' teachings are offered to a broad public. Chapters 13–21, particularly chapters 13–17, narrate Jesus' teaching and ministry to his disciples, those who have become the children of God.

Women disciples play significant roles in the Gospel of John. This is evident both in the number of stories in which women appear and in the doctrinal importance of those stories. Women are the main conversation partners in three stories that reveal Jesus' identity and calling and the nature of faithful discipleship.[35]

The opening miracle in Jesus' ministry occurs at a woman's initiative.[36] Jesus' suffering and death on the cross is watched over by women, from its preparation through his death and resurrection.[37] Women, as well as men, are disciples and witnesses of the risen Christ.

Mary, the mother of Jesus, is introduced in the story at the wedding of Cana and at the cross.[38] The accounts are similar because her name is omitted on both occasions; she is simply called the "mother of Jesus" and the "woman."[39] Jesus' concern for her, even at the end, shows not only his abiding love for her but also ultimately, his love for his faithful disciple.

John is the only Gospel writer to report Jesus' journey to Samaria, where he met the woman at the well, the first public announcement that he was the Messiah.[40]

In the following chapters, we will examine what each Gospel writer has to say about women and incidents or teachings involving women. Because we recognize the difficulties associated with narrative-type studies, as explained above, we have attempted to reduce those inherent difficulties by clearly identifying the contributions of each writer. While we suppose that much could be gained from focusing on each Gospel separately, that effort lies beyond the scope of this book.

Chapter Five

The Surprising Five:
The Women in Jesus' Genealogy

$\mathcal{T}$he Gospel of Matthew begins by dramatically announcing the genealogy of Jesus: "The book of the generation of Jesus Christ, the son of David, the son of Abraham."[1] Although genealogies were kept as early as the family of Adam, that practice must have fallen into disuse.[2] Many Jewish families, particularly after the exile in Babylon (ca. 538 B.C.), began again to keep genealogies. The keeping of genealogical records and family histories was important for all persons concerned with establishing their rights and protecting their property, but especially for those who wanted to qualify to hold a priestly or civic office.

The genealogical table is usually divided into three segments. First, from Abraham through the reign of David; second, from the rule of King Solomon to the collapse of the kingdom of Judah; and third, from the Exile to Babylon to Jesus' birth. Reviewing the material in this way is helpful, but for our purpose it is more important to focus on another aspect of the information that Matthew provided.

Matthew's genealogical list of Jesus' ancestors stretches from Abraham (founder of the Hebrew people) through Jacob to David (the second Hebrew king, who made Jerusalem the religious and political capital of Israel) and culminates with Joseph, "the husband of Mary."[3] By reciting the long list of Jesus' ancestors—Abraham, Isaac, Jacob, Judah, and all of the others for thirty-eight more generations—one is reminded of the long history of the Jewish people. The list in Matthew is unique in that it names five women. What is even more surprising is that these are five *atypical* women.

First is Thamar (the New Testament form of Tamar), the Canaanite wife of Judah's eldest son, Er. She was the woman who, with face veiled and by means of prostitution, deceived her father-in-law in order to perpetuate the lineage.[4] Rachab (the New Testament form of Rahab) was the prostitute who safeguarded Israel's spies upon entering Jericho.[5] Ruth was the Moabitess who married Boaz, a wealthy and virtuous Bethlehemite.[6] Bathsheba was the wife of Urias (the New Testament form of Uriah) with whom King David committed adultery.[7] The last of the five is Mary, a virgin who conceived before her formal marriage to Joseph.[8] Let us take a closer look at these five unusual women.

Tamar

Tamar married Judah's son Er. Because he "was wicked in the sight of the Lord," God "slew him."[9] When Judah's second son, Onan, refused to "raise up seed" to his deceased brother as was the custom, the Lord "slew him also."[10] At this point, Judah refused Tamar his third son "till Shelah my son grows up," because he feared for his son's life, suspecting Tamar was in some way responsible for the other two deaths.[11]

Tamar was sent back to live a widow in her father's house. Judah secretly considered this solution as final, but presented it to Tamar as an interim solution. Eventually she understood that Judah would not fulfill his obligation of providing a husband for her. So Tamar, acting for herself, "put her widow's garment off from her, and covered her with a veil, and wrapped herself, and sat in an open place."[12] Judah, suspecting her to be a prostitute, said, "Go to, I pray thee, let me come in unto thee; (for he knew not that she was his daughter in law.) And she said, What wilt thou give me, that thou mayest come in unto me?" Judah promised a "kid from the flock."[13] Tamar wanted a "pledge," so her father-in-law gave her his own signet, bracelets, and staff as security for the debt.[14]

Of course when Judah sent the payment, Tamar was gone, having returned to her own home. Sometime later Judah heard that his daughter-in-law "hath played the harlot; and also, behold, she is with child by whoredom."[15] He responded by accusing her and setting forth an appropriate punishment for her unfaithful conduct. "Bring her forth, and let her be burnt," he demanded.[16] At the last minute she produced Judah's personal effects to prove who the father of her unborn children was. Judah replied, "She hath been more righteous than I."[17] Thus the future royal lineage was continued through Judah when Tamar bore his twins, Perez and Zerah.

Rahab

Rahab's story begins in Joshua 2 when the Israelite leader "sent out . . . two men to spy secretly" to see the city of Jericho as the children of Israel began to invade the land promised to them.[18] When "they went," they "came into an harlot's house, named Rahab, and lodged there."[19] We are not informed why they came to her or why she received them; presumably her reputation attracted them, and she perhaps in turn welcomed them on the basis of her occupation.

"And it was told the king of Jericho, saying, Behold, there came men in hither to night of the children of Israel to search out the country. And the king of Jericho sent unto Rahab, saying, Bring forth the men that are come to thee, which are entered into thine house: for they be come to search out all the country."[20]

In a surprising move, Rahab defied the king and "took the two men, and hid them, and said thus, There came men unto me, but I wist not whence they were. . . . But she had brought them up to the roof of the house, and hid them with the stalks of flax, which she had laid in order upon the roof."[21]

Rahab told the men that she knew "that the Lord hath given you the land, and that your terror is fallen upon us, and that all the inhabitants of the land faint because of you. For we have heard how the Lord dried up the water of the Red sea for you, when ye came out of Egypt; and what ye did unto the two kings of the Amorites, that were on the other side Jordan, Sihon and Og, who ye utterly destroyed. And as soon as we had heard these things, our hearts did melt, neither did there remain any more courage in any man, because of you; for the Lord your God, he is God in heaven above, and in earth beneath."[22]

She obtained a promise from the spies that in return for her help she and her family would be saved when the city was conquered. Rahab let the spies down by a rope through a window in her apartment in the city wall. They then told her to bind a scarlet cord in that window when the spies returned with the army. When the city and all within it were destroyed, Joshua honored the promise: "And Joshua saved Rahab the harlot alive, and her father's household, and all that she had; and she dwelleth in Israel even unto this day; because she hid the messengers, which Joshua sent to spy out Jericho."[23] She, according to Matthew, became a progenitor of the Messiah.

Ruth

Ruth was a Moabite—an important aspect of the story as can be seen by the numerous times she is identified as such.[24] Descendants of Lot and his eldest daughter, the Moabites dwelt in the land east of the Dead Sea.[25] While akin to the Israelites, they were in constant warfare with them and were therefore despised and hated by all Israelites, including the Jews.[26]

During the time of the judges, a certain Israelite family from Bethlehem journeyed to Moab because of a harsh famine in the land. The father and then his two sons died (both having taken Moabite wives, Ruth and Orpah). Only the widowed mother, Naomi, and the two daughters-in-law remained. When Naomi decided to return to her native land, she bid the two young women to remain in Moab. Orpah consented, but Ruth clung to Naomi and requested to return with her to her home.

After their arrival in Bethlehem, the aged Naomi and the youthful Ruth struggled for survival without husbands to support them. Ruth gleaned in the fields of a wealthy man named Boaz who belonged to the extended family of her deceased father-in-law. His kindness prompted Naomi to plan a way for her widowed daughter-in-law to find a new husband, and therefore important security for them both. Obeying her mother-in-law, Ruth went to the threshing floor at night and asked Boaz to marry her:

> And she went down unto the floor, and did according to all that her mother in law bade her.

And when Boaz had eaten and drunk, and his heart was merry, he went to lie down at the end of the heap of corn: and she came softly, and uncovered his feet, and laid her down.

And it came to pass at midnight, that the man was afraid, and turned himself: and, behold, a woman lay at his feet.

And he said, Who art thou? And she answered, I am Ruth thine handmaid: spread therefore thy skirt over thine handmaid; for thou art a near kinsman.[27]

Though willing to fulfill the obligation of raising up seed to a dead relative, he had to first determine if a nearer relative wished to assume responsibility. The unnamed man refused, "So Boaz took Ruth, and she was his wife: and when he went in unto her, the Lord gave her conception, and she bare a son."[28] The son, Obed, was a blessing to his grandmother Naomi. His birth set in place his future position as the grandfather of King David.

Bathsheba

Our final Old Testament woman, Bathsheba, was the daughter of Eliam and the wife of Uriah the Hittite.[29] The story of David's adulterous affair with her, resulting in Bathsheba's pregnancy and David's stratagem to cause her husband's death and her eventual marriage to David, is one of the most well-known in the Bible.

From the palace rooftop David saw Bathsheba bathing. We are told nothing else about her except that she "was very beautiful."[30] David inquired about her and was informed about her marital status. The verbs used in the next verse are plain and blunt: "David *sent* messengers, and *took* her; and she came to him, and he *lay* with her."[31] The Joseph Smith Translation (JST, also known as the Inspired Version) of Matthew emphasizes the same, "And Jesse begat David the king; and David the king begat Solomon of her *whom David had taken of Urias.*"[32]

The straightforward talk continues: she returned home, learned that she had conceived, and sent word to David, "I am with child."[33]

David then plotted to bring Uriah home from battle with the hope that he would sleep with his wife and that the pregnancy would appear to be a result of their marital relations. When his plan failed, David next plotted and executed the murder of Uriah, in order to keep the adultery secret. What part Bathsheba played is not mentioned, only that "the thing that David had done displeased the Lord."[34] The reader is left to wonder if Bathsheba was victim or accomplice, or somehow both at once. She was seemingly entrapped in a situation where her feelings, rights, plans, and perhaps love—all counted for nothing.

In the incident that followed, Bathsheba played no part. The prophet Nathan confronted David with a parable about a poor man's little ewe lamb. Bathsheba, as wife of Uriah, was symbolized as a little ewe needlessly slaughtered. David, not discerning the symbolism, judged that the rich man who took the lamb deserved death, but he designated instead a monetary penalty for the crime. David's judgment indicates that the issue was not simply theft (or adultery) but rather of a lack of pity, compassion, sympathy, and even physical mercy that would spare a potential victim from some form of violence.[35]

David, both by implication of the parable's symbolism and by very deed, showed no pity for Bathsheba. Nathan condemned David, saying, "Thou art the man."[36] In punishment, David was told that evil would be raised up against him out of his own house. David did not die for his transgression, but the child born to him and Bathsheba did. Then "David comforted Bathsheba his wife, and went in unto her, and lay with her: and she bare a son, and he called his name Solomon: and the Lord loved him."[37]

Bathsheba appears again in 1 Kings 1, when David was near death. Nathan sent her to David to remind him that David had promised that Solomon would be king, rather than Adonijah, his eldest. David then bent to her will, as she had once bent to his.

Mary

The last woman mentioned in Matthew's version of Jesus' genealogy is of course Mary, the mother of Jesus. Marriage customs of the day would imply that Mary was a young girl of not more than twelve or thirteen years of age when she became engaged to Joseph. Before "they came together, she was found with child."[38] To avoid the embarrassment of a public hearing to determine if his young bride-to-be had been seduced or raped, Joseph decided to instead "put her away privily."[39]

As Joseph thought about the situation, "the angel of the Lord appeared unto him in a dream, saying, Joseph, thou son of David, fear not to take unto thee Mary thy wife."[40] The angel told him that Mary would bring forth a son and that he should call his name Jesus. According to Matthew, "this was done, that it might be fulfilled which was spoken of the Lord by the prophet, saying, Behold, a virgin shall be with child, and shall bring forth a son, and they shall call his name Emmanuel, which being interpreted is God with us."[41]

Why These Women Are Included

When the names are reviewed, it is surprising that Matthew mentions five women, whereas Luke records only men in Jesus' genealogy.[42] Why did Matthew mention these five women in particular? One might expect the names of the Hebrew matriarchs (Sarah, Rebekah, and Rachel), but instead Matthew has unexpectedly included the names of these five unusual women. What do these women have in common to explain their inclusion? There are several possibilities.[43]

The first theory asserts that Matthew is attempting to demonstrate that Jesus has come to save sinners and that Tamar, Rahab, and Bathsheba foreshadowed Jesus' role of saving sinners. This seems somewhat unsatisfactory since Matthew himself states, "And she shall bring forth a son, and thou shalt call his name Jesus: for he shall *save his people* from their sins."[44] Matthew implies that Jesus will bring redemption to all, not just these particular women in the genealogy who no more symbolize sinners in need of redemption than the men.

The Bible itself does not identify the four Old Testament women as sinners, nor would it seem that Matthew considered Mary a sinner. More particularly, rabbinic traditions during Jesus' lifetime suggest that these four Old Testament women were esteemed. Tamar was considered a heroine by Jesus' contemporaries for taking the initiative in perpetuating the line of Judah's son, her deceased husband. According to Jewish tradition, she did this because she had great faith in the messianic promise concerning Judah's lineage.

Likewise, Rahab, classified a convert to Judaism, was considered a heroine for protecting the Israelite spies in Jericho and thus assuring Joshua's victory over the city. Bathsheba's adultery, the rabbis argued, was not condemned because she ultimately gave birth to Solomon.[45] It seems unlikely that Matthew or his first-century Jewish Christian audience would have considered these women sinners, which would have made a connection between them and Jesus' mission untenable.

Another view suggests that since Rahab and Ruth were Gentiles, their presence (along with that of Uriah the Hittite) foresaw the welcoming of Gentiles into the Church, or at least that it was an attempt to show that the Jewish Messiah was related by ancestry to the Gentiles. Rahab and possibly Tamar were thought to be Canaanites, and Ruth was a Moabite. Bathsheba's origin is not noted in the biblical record, but it is as "the wife of Urias" the Hittite that Matthew describes her. A Gentile connection seems somewhat reasonable but admittedly tenuous.

Jewish tradition suggests that Rahab was considered a proselyte (from the Greek word meaning "to draw near") or convert to Judaism.[46] The Bible indicates that Ruth was a convert. Anticipation of the Gentile mission therefore is confused by including these women, because Gentile Christians did not have to become Jews first before becoming Christians. In first-century Jewish literature, Tamar and Bathsheba were usually considered to be Hebrews. Nor can a Gentile association explain Mary's presence in this group of five women, since she was not a Gentile herself.

Another view holds that Matthew has included the first four women as a means of preparing the reader for the story of Mary that follows. Matthew, according to this proposition, is attempting to combat Jewish charges of the illegitimate birth of Jesus and therefore focuses on the extramarital sexual activity of the other women in the royal line as a means of defusing such accusations. The four sinners in the Davidic line, according to this argument, are to be contrasted with the sinless Mary. It is certain that such charges were in circulation at the time. Mark may have recorded such an accusation when Jesus returned to "his own country" and "began to teach in the synagogue."[47] The audience was surprised, and said: "From whence hath this man these things? and what wisdom is this which is given unto him, that even such mighty works are wrought by his hands? Is not this the carpenter, the son of Mary . . . ?" After reporting what the people said, the record then states, "And they were offended at him."[48]

To describe a Jewish man as the "son of" his mother, even when the father was deceased, was an insult because Jews were customarily known by their father's name (such as "son of Joseph"). This may be an insinuation of Jesus' illegitimacy by local townspeople. On another occasion when Jesus talked about his Father, the Jews replied, "We be not born of fornication."[49] Here the Jews may be turning to a well-known argument against Jesus. He has been talking about his Father in Heaven and about their father, but rumors about his own birth questioned whether Jesus was really the son of Joseph. The Jews may be saying in effect, "We were not born of fornication [but you were]."

Basically, the first- and second-century anti-Jesus controversy can be summarized as follows: Jesus in the New Testament was the illegitimate son of an adulterous Jewish woman and a Roman soldier named Pandera or Panthere. Later rabbinic sources, such as the fifth-century Talmud, which scholars believe referred to Jesus and his mother, stated: "But his mother was Miriam [Mary is the English equivalent for the New Testament name], the hairdresser. . . , 'this one has been unfaithful to her husband.'"[50] To be sure, such rumors and accusations abounded in anti-Christian propaganda of the period, and it may well have played a part in including this particular birth narrative in Matthew's Gospel. All three views may well have contributed to Matthew's design, but another aspect should be considered too.

There is one element that all five women seemed to share. While considered disgraceful by those who could not see the hand of God, the unions they entered into played an important role in God's divine plan. Tamar took the initiative in bringing about her somewhat shocking union with Judah and therefore became the mother of the kings of Israel. Rahab's life as a prostitute suggests another unusual aspect of these women, yet her help to the Israelite spies not only saved her household but also made her a progenitor of their future Messiah. The marriage of Ruth was certainly irregular and was brought about by Ruth's initiative. Without that initiative, the Davidic line might not have come into being. It was through Bathsheba's intervention that Solomon succeeded David as the King of Israel.[51]

In rabbinical Judaism, these extraordinary unions and initiatives were seen as examples of how God used the unexpected to triumph over seemingly impossible obstacles. The mention of the first four women is designed to lead Matthew's audience to expect another, final story of an unusual woman. In this, Matthew might have chosen these particular women as a means of foreshadowing Mary's own experience, something totally unexpected. *If God could work through these four women, why not through Mary?* In Mary's situation, the intervention was even greater than in those already mentioned. All five of the women whom Matthew mentioned represent undeniable faith in the future and courage during the present. Each in her own way played an important role in preparing the way for the birth of the mortal Messiah.

Chapter Six

The First Believers:
Elisabeth, Mary, and Anna

*I*n Luke, three women—Elisabeth, Mary, and Anna—are reminiscent of Old Testament women blessed with the gifts of the Spirit, such as Miriam and Deborah. These women play powerful roles unlike anything else found in the four Gospels.

Elisabeth (Luke 1:5–25, 39–45, 56–63)

Luke's story begins in the "days of Herod, the king of Judaea [the New Testament form of Judah]."[1] Zacharias (the New Testament form of Zachariah) and Elisabeth (the New Testament form of Elisheba—Aaron's wife had the same name) are childless.[2] Because Jewish society believed that barrenness was a misfortune, even a disgrace or a punishment for wickedness and sin, Luke states, "They were both righteous before God, walking in all the commandments and ordinances of the Lord blameless."[3]

Elisabeth is mentioned only in the first chapter of Luke, which states that she was a descendant of Aaron, barren and advanced in years. Like several Old Testament women, the barrenness and divine intervention that subsequently causes Elisabeth to become pregnant are signs that she will bear a child important in Israel's history.[4] Elisabeth and Sarah are especially similar in that they were not only barren but also beyond normal child-bearing age.[5] This makes God's intervention all the more miraculous.

For Luke, Elisabeth is a model of faith, as evidenced by the fact that this story focuses on her perspective, not Zacharias's. In fact, this fact is but the first of many reversals of ordinary expectations in this story; for example, Elisabeth, not Zacharias, properly responds to God's announcement. She and Mary are the first to receive the message of the coming of the Messiah, the first to respond in full faith to that news, the first to be praised and blessed by God's angels, and the first to sing and prophesy about the Christ child.

When Mary visited her relative in "a city of Juda—the hill country," Elisabeth pronounced a twofold blessing upon her.[6] To capture the unrestrained joy, Luke states that she blessed Mary with a "loud voice"—literally, with a great cry. First, she blessed Mary because she would be the mother of her Lord.[7] Second, she blessed Mary above all because she responded in faith to the previously revealed words of an angel: she believed the promise given to her about the coming of the Messiah.[8] Luke indicates that Elisabeth is also to be seen as something of a prophetess[9]: "And it came to pass, that, when Elisabeth heard the salutation of Mary, the babe leaped in her womb; and Elisabeth was filled with the Holy Ghost. And she spake out with a loud voice, and said, Blessed art thou among women, and blessed is the fruit of thy womb."[10]

Mary's mere salutation caused the baby to leap in Elisabeth's womb. What the angel promised Zacharias earlier was thus fulfilled.[11] Elisabeth was given not only inspired insight into the mission of the baby in Mary's womb and into the events that had just transpired in Mary's life but also the power to interpret the sign of her own child leaping in her womb. She acknowledged both the baby in Mary's womb as her "Lord" and also Mary as the "mother of the Lord." The beautiful blessing she uttered, the Song of Elisabeth, is a hymn of praise:

> Blessed art thou among women, and blessed is the fruit of thy womb.
>
> And whence is this to me, that the mother of my Lord should come to me?
>
> For, lo, as soon as the voice of thy salutation sounded in mine ears, the babe leaped in my womb for joy.
>
> And blessed is she that believed: for there shall be a performance of those things which were told her from the Lord.[12]

After Mary had lived with her cousin for three months, she returned home. Luke continues his story:

> Now Elisabeth's full time came that she should be delivered; and she brought forth a son.
> And her neighbours and her cousins heard how the Lord had shewed great mercy upon her; and they rejoiced with her.
> And it came to pass, that on the eighth day they came to circumcise the child; and they called him Zacharias, after the name of his father.
> And his mother answered and said, Not so; but he shall be called John.
> And they said unto her, There is none of thy kindred that is called by this name.
> And they made signs to his father, how he would have him called.
> And he asked for a writing table, and wrote, saying, His name is John.[13]

It is significant that Elisabeth gave her child his name when he was born, an act which Zacharias only confirmed.

Mary (Luke 1:26–56; 2:1–19; Matthew 1:18–25)

In the same chapter of Luke, we are also introduced to another woman, Mary (the New Testament form of Miriam). The mother of Jesus is an important figure in the four Gospels (even though John never referred to her by name). Luke depicted Mary as the model female believer and preserved two important stories about Mary for us—the annunciation of Jesus' birth and the birth itself.[14]

In stark contrast to the story of the annunciation of John's birth to an elderly married couple, Mary is presented as a young virgin, only betrothed to Joseph.[15] When the angel of the Lord appeared to her, she was living at home in Nazareth, "a city of Galilee," about fifteen miles west of the Sea of Galilee (also known as Lake Gennesaret or Tiberias) and twenty miles east of the Mediterranean.[16]

Nazareth is not mentioned in the Old Testament. Like Bethlehem, Bethsaida, Nain, and Sychar, it probably did not deserve to be called "a city." Nazareth was, along with these other towns and villages, very insignificant during Jesus' lifetime.[17] And unlike Jerusalem, it was unwalled and small, with boxlike houses huddled close together on the side of a small hill, some distance from the main road. At the highest point stood a simple one-story synagogue. Most of its two hundred inhabitants were farmers, but a few worked as craftsmen, like Joseph.

Mary's role as the "highly favored" one (that is, the mother of Jesus) is the basis for our viewing her as a disciple who hears and responds to God's word.[18] This is alluded to during Jesus' ministry: "And it came to pass, as he spake these things, a certain woman of the company lifted up her voice, and said unto him, Blessed is the womb that bare thee, and the paps which thou hast sucked." Jesus responded, "Yea rather, blessed are they that hear the word of God and keep it."[19] In other words, Mary was blessed for hearing and keeping God's word, just as all are required to do.

During this period in Jewish Palestine, the marriage of a young girl took place in two distinct stages. First came the formal exchange in the presence of witnesses when the betrothed agreed to marry and the groom paid the bride price. During this stage, the prospective spouses are set apart for each other: they are betrothed, that is, "hallowed" or "sanctified" (which is what "set apart" means in Hebrew/Aramaic). Remember that marriage in Jewish Palestine during the first century was made between extended families, not individuals, and was arranged by parents; there were no agreements between a man and a woman who were romantically attracted to each other.

The usual age of a girl's betrothal was between twelve and twelve and a half; that is, at puberty or a little before. The engagement constituted a legally ratified marriage, since it began her transfer from her father's authority to her husband's, giving the latter legal rights over her and giving her the status of a married woman for many purposes. She could be called his wife or become his widow.[20]

The betrothal, which lasted about a year, could be broken only by the husband's divorcing his new wife. If she were to violate any of his marital rights during this period (when she continued to live in her father's house), her actions would be considered adultery. The second stage was the wedding proper, the transfer of the young girl to her husband's home, where he assumed her support. Only at this point did she definitely and fully pass to her husband's authority.

The young girl was normally assumed to be a virgin at the time of her betrothal, and, at least in Galilee, also at the time of her marriage. Under a more lenient custom in Judaea, a charge of adultery could not be lodged if her betrothed had ever been alone with her (the assumption was that they could have had sexual relations with each other). The reason for this difference was due to the fact that the occupying Roman troops might rape or seduce a betrothed virgin.

Joseph must have discovered Mary's pregnancy between their betrothal and completed marriage, before she and Joseph "came together," probably meaning before Mary was brought to Joseph's home. Joseph's reaction, according to Matthew, makes it plain that he was not the biological father.[21] "Joseph was a just man"—that is, Torah observant—and "not willing to make her a publick example," so he "minded to put her away privily [secretly]," that is, in the presence of chosen witnesses and without public scandal.[22]

The only two logical explanations for Mary's condition were adultery or rape. Nevertheless, Joseph chose not to have a public hearing to determine whether Mary had been seduced or raped. In deciding against the hearing, he was shielding her and himself not only from the public shame and questioning involved in the hearing but also from the possibility of an accusation and conviction on the charge of seduction or adultery.

Such a conviction could result either in death by stoning as the law of Moses demanded or more likely in a degrading divorce (which was the only way to end the betrothal), perhaps with attendant indignities (such as physical and emotional abuses) and certainly with a bleak future for Mary.[23] Among the abuses a young woman was exposed to was a series of curses chanted by the people of the village: "Cursed be he who begot her, cursed be he who brought her up, cursed be he from whose loins she sprang."[24] Joseph chose the kindest and most humane alternative that the law offered.

Not until the angel told Joseph to take Mary as his wife did he understand that a third explanation of the situation was actually the correct one.[25] A Torah-observant man who completed the *home-taking* (the final act of the marriage cycle) could also adopt the child of his wife into his family. Joseph, by accepting the pregnant Mary into his home, accepted responsibility for the child she was carrying. The angelic words, "Thou shalt call his name Jesus," are equivalent to a formula of adoption.[26] Joseph, by exercising the father's right to name the child, acknowledged Jesus and thus became his adoptive and legal father.

When the angel of the Lord first appeared to the young Mary, she was perhaps not more than twelve years of age and almost certainly not more than fourteen years of age:

> And in the sixth month the angel Gabriel was sent from God unto a city of Galilee, named Nazareth,
>
> To a virgin espoused to a man whose name was Joseph, of the house of David; and the virgin's name was Mary.
>
> And the angel came in unto her, and said, Hail, thou that art highly favoured, the Lord is with thee: blessed art thou among women.
>
> And when she saw him, she was troubled at his saying, and cast in her mind what manner of salutation this should be.
>
> And the angel said unto her, Fear not, Mary: for thou hast found favour with God.
>
> And, behold, thou shalt conceive in thy womb, and bring forth a son, and shalt call his name JESUS.[27]

Mary's reaction may be the natural result of what any mortal might experience in the unexpected presence of a divine being, or in a Jewish cultural context, a maiden's reaction to the presence of man, or a combination of both. While Matthew records that Joseph is told by an angel in a dream what to name the baby, Luke is careful to show that Mary is also commanded to name the child, thus placing her with other divinely favored Old Testament female precedents.[28]

The Joseph Smith Translation (JST) of the Bible adds a few significant details to Luke's version of the incident: "And the angel came in unto her, and said, Hail, thou *virgin*, who art highly favoured *of the Lord*, the Lord is with thee: *for thou art chosen* and blessed among women. And when she saw the angel, she was troubled at his saying, and *pondered* in her mind what manner of salutation this should be."[29]

Mary questioned the messenger, "How shall this be, seeing I

know not a man?"[30] Of course, "I know not a man" is a eu-
phemism that means "I have not had sexual relations with a man."
The angel informed her that "the power of the Highest shall over-
shadow thee: therefore also that holy thing which shall be born of
thee shall be called the Son of God."[31] She, as a model of discipleship, replied, "Behold the handmaid of the Lord; be it unto me
according to thy word."[32]

The traditional focus on Mary as the Lord's mortal mother
has obscured her other role as Jesus' first disciple. Her discipleship
began on one Spirit-filled occasion. Mary called herself a handmaid—servant or, more technically correct, "slave." As a result,
some may view Mary as a passive individual, such as a slave. Since
slaves held the lowest social position within Greco-Roman society
and were without any legal protection, unable to own property, or
have a family or a genealogy in the proper sense, Mary has been
seen as a model of feminine submissive behavior; therefore, some
reason, she accepted the belief that women were inferior, dependent, and helpless.

There is another way to read the passage, however. For Luke
the term *slave* seems to have a positive significance. It must be
seen in connection with Jewish usage of the honorary title "slave
of God," applied to a few outstanding men of Israelite history
(Abraham, Isaac, Jacob, Moses, Joshua, David, Solomon, and the
prophets) and one woman (Hannah).[33] The Old Testament's use
of "slave" language is thus continued in Luke when Mary accepts
this special and honored relationship to God.

This designation also associates Mary with Jesus, portrayed
among the disciples "as he that serveth," and with the female
slaves (handmaids) on whom God's Spirit would be poured, making them prophets:[34] "And it shall come to pass afterward, that I
will pour out my spirit upon all flesh; and your sons and your
daughters shall prophesy, your old men shall dream dreams, your
young men shall see visions: And also upon the servants and upon
the *handmaids* in those days will I pour out my spirit."[35]

Mary's own hymn of praise is not the song of a Greco-Roman
slave—a victim of a brutal system—but one that proclaims libera-
tion.[36] In answer to Elisabeth's praise of her, Mary uttered her
praise of God for what had happened to her.[37] She compared
"God my Saviour" who "is mighty" with her own "low estate":[38]

And Mary said, My soul doth magnify the Lord,
And my spirit hath rejoiced in God my Saviour.
For he hath regarded the low estate of his handmaiden: for, be-
hold, from henceforth all generations shall call me blessed.
For he that is mighty hath done to me great things; and holy is
his name.
And his mercy is on them that fear him from generation to gen-
eration.
He hath shewed strength with his arm; he hath scattered the
proud in the imagination of their hearts.
He hath put down the mighty from their seats, and exalted
them of low degree.
He hath filled the hungry with good things; and the rich he
hath sent empty away.
He hath holpen [helped] his servant Israel, in remembrance of
his mercy;
As he spake to our fathers, to Abraham, and to his seed for
ever.[39]

This beautiful song of thanksgiving demonstrates great spiritual insight for a twelve- or thirteen-year-old girl. Like Hannah of
old, the once-barren woman whose condition was reversed and
who became the mother of Samuel, Mary extolled the Lord's
greatness, might, holiness, and mercy.[40] Mary's song of praise also
can be compared to similar psalms in the Old Testament.[41]

Mary praised the past great deeds of the Lord God of Israel
and gave thanks for the new manifestation of God's power in the
conception of the child to be born to her. She recognized that the
salvation that was to come through her son's birth, life, and mission was related to the covenant made by God with Abraham of old.

Her status as a disciple can also be demonstrated by compar-
ing the angel's words, "the power of the Highest shall over-
shadow thee," with the words Luke used to describe Peter, James,
and John's experience upon the Mount of Transfiguration.[42] Both
texts refer to "a cloud, *shekinah* of the Hebrew Old Testament,
being a sign of God's presence."[43] Both are brought into God's
presence by being "overshadowed," and both refer to God's witness of Jesus' divine sonship.

After Mary's visit with Elisabeth, she returned home.[44] Sometime later, "in those days," Mary journeyed with Joseph to Bethlehem, a small village of no more than three hundred people at

the time and made up of a cluster of boxlike, whitewashed houses on the top of a low but rather steep ridge.

> There went out a decree from Caesar Augustus, that all the world should be taxed.
> (And this taxing was first made when Cyrenius was governor of Syria.)
> And all went to be taxed, every one into his own city.
> And Joseph also went up from Galilee, out of the city of Nazareth, into Judaea, unto the city of David, which is called Bethlehem; (because he was of the house and lineage of David:)
> To be taxed with Mary his espoused wife, being great with child.[45]

Three hundred years later, when the Roman Emperor Diocletian, ordered a census of the entire empire for the purpose of assessing a head tax, women were counted, but not as the equivalent of men; on rural estates in Thrace (modern eastern Greece), for example, two women counted as one man. Before that, women had not been counted at all. So Luke emphasized the role Joseph plays in the taxing, since Mary and other women of Jewish Palestine were not counted for taxing.

The normal rate of travel for the time would have brought Mary and Joseph to Bethlehem late in the afternoon of their fifth day of the journey. They would have walked about eighty miles from Nazareth, accompanied by a donkey to carry their supplies. "And so it was, that, while they were there, the days were accomplished that she should be delivered. And she brought forth her firstborn son."[46] Mary probably gave birth to Jesus in the Roman year 747, or 6 B.C. by our modern calendar. Luke continued his story, "And [she] wrapped him in swaddling clothes [in a tight bundle], and laid him in a manger; because there was no room for them in the inn."[47]

There is no reason to assume that they arrived in Bethlehem immediately before the infant's birth. Bethlehem almost certainly had no inns, being a small village and only a two-hour walk from Jerusalem. Although the Greek word here translated as "inn" can sometimes mean an inn, it normally refers to a large furnished room attached to a home and is best translated "guest room."

The only other use of this term in the New Testament is in the story of the Last Supper where it is translated "guestchamber."[48] The normal word for inn is used in Luke 10:34; such an inn was a place that "receives all." The fact that there was no "place" for Joseph and Mary in the guest room of the home probably meant that it was already occupied by someone who in all likelihood outranked them socially.

A house was soon found, however, that allowed them to stay temporarily in the manger. Simple homes of the period consisted of one room, though sometimes a guest room would have been attached. The family usually occupied one end of the main room (often raised) and the animals the other. A manger was located in between.

Much of the attention given to newborns was misguided by today's standards and not conducive to their overall health. As was the practice of the day, Mary, or a midwife who may have been present, would have washed Jesus with salt, possibly combined with honey and olive oil, and then bathed him in lukewarm water. But the swaddling that would have immediately followed and continued for around three months was not a health practice. The purpose of wrapping an infant tightly in cloth may have been to provide strength and security and to ensure a straight, strong, healthy body. Nevertheless, for Luke, the manger and the swaddling clothes were important signs.[49]

> And there were in the same country shepherds abiding in the field, keeping watch over their flock by night.
> And, lo, the angel of the Lord came upon them, and the glory of the Lord shone round about them: and they were sore afraid.
> And the angel said unto them, Fear not: for, behold, I bring you good tidings of great joy, which shall be to all people.
> For unto you is born this day in the city of David a Saviour, which is Christ the Lord.
> And this shall be a sign unto you; Ye shall find the babe wrapped in swaddling clothes, lying in a manger.[50]

Like Zacharias and Mary, the shepherds received a sign to confirm the angelic announcement. It was an unusual one, corresponding in no way to the signs that one might have expected of a coming Messiah.[51] The manger (actually a feeding trough for animals) was referred to a third time: "And they came with haste, and found Mary, and Joseph, and the babe lying in a manger."[52] They found the child wrapped in cloth bands in a manger where Mary had laid him. This description of Jesus' birth contrasts sharply with the Jewish expectation of a Davidic Messiah who was to restore the kingdom to Israel politically and perhaps militarily.[53]

"And when [the shepherds] had seen it, they made known abroad [to Mary and Joseph and undoubtedly to the inhabitants of Bethlehem too] the saying which was told them concerning this child. And all they that heard it wondered [were surprised] at those things which were told them by the shepherds."[54] When the shepherds had left, Luke states, "Mary kept all these things" (literally, "she preserved all these words") and "pondered them in her heart."[55]

Mary already knew that her child was the promised Messiah and that he had been recognized by the angel Gabriel as Lord.[56] Maybe the shepherds' visit coupled with their story of angelic ministration was an unexpected surprise. The episode finally ends with the departure of the shepherds, who return to their flocks, echoing the song of the angels in their praise and glorifying of God.

The next recorded episode begins when Jesus was eight days old: "And when eight days were accomplished for the circumcising of the child, his name was called Jesus, which was so named of the angel before he was conceived in the womb,"[57] referring to Mary's experience. While the King James Version (KJV) of Matthew indicates that Joseph gave the name, the Joseph Smith Translation (JST) emphasizes, "and *they* called his name Jesus."[58]

There is undoubtedly a correlation between the eight-day period between birth and circumcision and the duration of the initial period of the mother's impurity after giving birth to a male child.[59] When the second phase of her impurity was complete (a total of forty days), Mary went to the temple to present an offering in obedience to the Levitical precept that required "a pair of turtledoves, or two young pigeons." Apparently young Joseph and Mary could not afford the one-year-old lamb required, so they substituted the birds in its place.[60]

The trip to Jerusalem from nearly any location was difficult for a new mother. Elevation changes in Jewish Palestine were significant, and each step ascending towards Jerusalem was a strenuous one, even through the temple itself. Jerusalem, it must be remembered, is 2,600 feet above the Mediterranean and the Sea of Galilee is nearly 700 feet below sea level.

Mary came to the holy city and then to the temple with her husband and new son. As first-century Jewish historian Flavius Josephus makes clear, the temple layout itself consisted of progressively more restricted courtyards, culminating in the Holy of Holies. "It had several courts, encompassed with cloisters round about, every one of which had by our law a peculiar degree of separation from the rest. Into the first court everybody was allowed to go, even foreigners [Gentiles]; and none but women, during their courses [menstruation], were prohibited to pass through it; all the Jews went into the second court, as well as their wives, when they were free from all uncleanness; into the third went the Jewish men when they were clean and purified; into the fourth went the priests."[61]

As for the Holy of Holies, only the high priest in his special robe could enter on the Yom Kippur—the Day of Atonement. Josephus also indicated that even the gates were segregated, for women could enter the "court of women" only through the south and north gates, and they were "not admitted through the [gates] nor allowed to go past the dividing wall with their own gate."[62] By the time Jesus' ministry began, gone were the days when women tended "the door of the tabernacle."[63]

It is not hard to imagine the events surrounding Mary's visit to the temple. She and Joseph were likely immersed in one of the public pools before nightfall. It might have been one of the forty-eight *miqva'ot* (*miqveh*, singular)—ritual immersion pools—recently found alongside the temple esplanade in Jerusalem.[64]

The next morning, Joseph, Mary, and Jesus would have gone to the temple. They would have entered the temple through the eastern gate in the southern wall and emerged into the Court of the Gentiles, where the moneychangers located their tables for business each day.

Anyone could enter this portion of the Temple Mount, including non-Jews. Walking to the royal portico, they would have found baskets or bowls, each containing two inspected birds to buy for the woman's offering after childbirth. They would have then crossed the Court of the Gentiles and come to the balustrade that warned Gentiles to go no further. This sign, painted in red letters and prominently displayed on the wall before one entered the

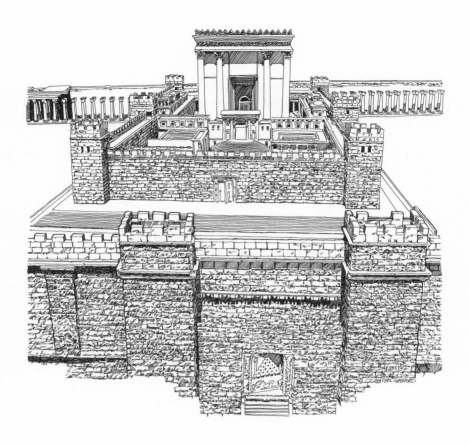

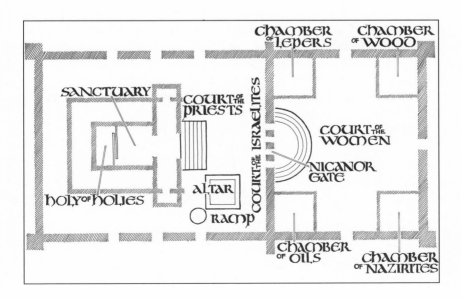

CHAMBER OF THE LEPERS

CHAMBER OF WOOD

SANCTUARY

COURT OF THE PRIESTS

COURT OF THE ISRAELITES

COURT OF THE WOMEN

NICANOR GATE

HOLY OF HOLIES

ALTAR

RAMP

CHAMBER OF OILS

CHAMBER OF NAZIRITES

Court of Women, read: "No foreigner [Gentile] is to enter within the forecourt and the balustrade around the sanctuary. Whoever is caught will have himself to blame for his subsequent death."[65]

Here at this entrance they would have assured one of the Levites on duty that they were pure. At some point, probably at the inner wall, they would have separated, Mary and Jesus going off to enter the Court of Women, and Joseph walking straight through the first eastern gate by going up a low flight of steps through the gate itself (called Beautiful Gate because of its elaborate decorations). Near the entrance to the Court of Women, Mary would have found a Levite and given him her birds, explaining that they were a sin offering for childbirth. She would have then entered and gone upstairs into a gallery to watch while the Levite found a priest, who then sacrificed the two birds.

The court itself comprised nearly two hundred square feet and was surrounded by porticoes. It was a place of meeting and discussing the scriptures and the events of the day. Against the walls inside the porticoes were thirteen repositories for the temple treasury, each one shaped like a shofar, or ram's horn trumpet, and open to receive offerings given to defray the costs of sacrifice. Here the widow cast in her two mites.[66] It was also in this location that Jesus dealt mercifully with the adulterous woman.[67]

They may have watched for a while, at least until the sacrifice was completed. Although sacrifice was a normal and standard part of worship, it was not a routine activity. Most residents of Jewish Palestine probably sacrificed on only a few occasions each year. The act was surrounded by awe. The majesty of the setting, the physical actions—selecting the sacrifice, seeing the Levite pass the birds or animals to a priest, and finally the sacrifice itself—guaranteed the moment's meaning and wonder.

The temple was indeed an awesome structure. According to Josephus, the outside of the structure was adorned with so much gold that when the sun shone upon it, it virtually blinded those who looked at it.[68]

Anna (Luke 2:36–38)

While Mary, Joseph, and Jesus were in the temple, a third woman appears in the story—an elderly and especially devout Jewish widow. "And there was one Anna [the New Testament form of Hannah], a prophetess, the daughter of Phanuel, of the tribe of Aser [the New Testament form of Asher]."[69] This is the only woman identified as a prophetess in the four Gospels. Whether a special sort of Jewish order of widows with specific functions in the temple existed at this time is not clear. In all likelihood, Anna met the young couple and their child in the Court of Women.

Luke informs us that she was a widow over one hundred years of age.[70] This is quite remarkable, because nearly 90 percent of the population at the time died by their mid-forties.

Luke may have also intended us to think of her as one of the righteous poor whom the Messiah would redeem—one of Luke's common themes.[71] He also stresses the fact that she continually fasted and prayed in the temple (presumably in the Court of Women). When she entered the area where Mary, Joseph, and Jesus were in the temple, she "gave thanks likewise unto the Lord, and spake of him to all them that looked for redemption in Jerusalem."[72]

Anna's words have not been preserved, although Luke states that she "gave thanks likewise" (referring to the words of Simeon who had preceded her) and also "spake of him." Anna then went forth to proclaim the good news about the Messiah. Both Anna and Simeon gave Mary something to ponder. After Simeon (possibly a Levitical priest) blessed Mary, he said to her, "Behold, this child is set for the fall and rising again of many in Israel; and for a sign which shall be spoken against; (Yea, a sword shall pierce through thy own soul also,) that the thoughts of many hearts may be revealed."[73] Mary, Joseph, and Jesus then returned home.

Mary, Joseph, and the Child (Matthew 2:1–23; Luke 2:42–52)

It seems that the couple and their baby lived in or around Bethlehem for at least two years following Jesus' birth. It is possible that Joseph owned a small piece of land in the area and decided not to return to Nazareth. The fact that Joseph came to Bethlehem to be enrolled implies that he had land there (hence, family), because the census or enrollment was for land taxation. During some point while living or staying in Bethlehem, the next recorded episode of significance in Mary's life unfolds:

> There came wise men from the east to Jerusalem.
>   . . . And, lo, the star, which they saw in the east, went before
> them, till it came and stood over where the young child was.
>   When they saw the star, they rejoiced with exceeding great joy.
>   And when they were come into *the house*, they saw the young
> child with Mary his mother, and fell down, and worshipped him: and
> when they had opened their treasures, they presented unto him gifts;
> gold, and frankincense, and myrrh.[74]

The wise men are not described as Gentiles or kings, nor does Matthew say that they are three in number. Their coming to Mary's *house* seems to indicate that this is a residence, and because Herod ordered the young children "two years old and under" to be killed, Mary, Joseph, and Jesus apparently lived in Bethlehem for at least one year.[75]

Shortly after their visit, Joseph was warned in a dream to flee to Egypt to avoid Herod's wrath.[76] The gifts, particularly the gold, may have financed Mary and Joseph's departure into Egypt and their survival there until their return to Jewish Palestine following Herod's death.

"Then Herod . . . slew all the children that were in Bethlehem, and in all the coast thereof."[77] The term *coast* in the Gospels refers to borders or boundaries of a certain region. Matthew saw this atrocious act as the fulfillment of Hebrew prophecy from Jeremiah: "In Rama [the New Testament form of Ramah] was there a voice heard, lamentation, and weeping, and great mourning, Rachel weeping for her children, and would not be comforted, because they are not.[78]

Mary's own discipleship began when the angel of the Lord first appeared to her, and it grew as she learned the cost of discipleship in following her son. It became more challenging as the young child escaped a death threat from the king. More particularly she understood that cost as the adult Jesus became hated, persecuted, and brutally executed. Her discipleship grew as she came to know, love, and follow her son as her Master and Redeemer. As Elisabeth and Anna disappeared from view, Mary continued to play a role in the four Gospel narratives, but not as dominant as she played in both Matthew and in the first two chapters of Luke.

The family returned after some time to Jewish Palestine, but not to Bethlehem where Jesus was born. Joseph took his adopted son and Mary back to Galilee, an area rich in farmlands with towns and villages numbering just over two hundred. They settled in Nazareth, and from this point until Jesus reached the age of twelve, not much is known of the family. We assume that like any mother of the period, Mary watched over and cared for her son the best she knew how.

It must be remembered that at the time some 28 percent of all newborn infants died before they reached one year of age, and around 50 percent died before the age of ten.[79] Childhood in antiquity was often a time of terror because children always suffered first from famine, war, disease, and dislocation; and in some areas or eras, few would have lived to adulthood with both parents alive.

When the twelve-year-old Jesus and his parents went "up to Jerusalem" for the Passover festival, called the Feast of Unleavened Bread, they followed Jewish tradition.[80] This important feast was one of three (the other two were the Feast of Tabernacles and the Feast of Weeks) to which Israelite men were commanded to appear before the Lord, by presenting themselves at the temple.[81]

Passover was celebrated at the end of the winter (our springtime). The trip up to Jerusalem was one of celebration and joy as the pilgrims arrived near the holy city. The days could be sunny and beautiful, but the nights could still be cold. The city, normally having between thirty-five and fifty thousand inhabitants, was of course crowded from the additional host of pilgrims.

Mary went as an observer, since women were permitted to accompany the male members of their family but could not participate in the duties men performed at the temple. After the celebration, Joseph and Mary began their return trip to Nazareth, going "a day's journey" before discovering that young Jesus was not with the company.[82]

When they returned to Jerusalem, they found him in the temple. Jesus was most likely in the temple's eastern portico, called Solomon's Porch, which overlooks the Kidron Valley.[83] This colonnaded area, like the others that surrounded the temple precinct, provided a meeting place for individuals to discuss scripture with leading Jewish scribes and rabbis of the day:

> And when they saw him, they were amazed: and his mother said unto him, Son, why hast thou thus dealt with us? behold, thy father and I have sought thee sorrowing.

And he said unto them, How is it that ye sought me? wist [knew] ye not that I must be about my Father's business?

And they understood not the saying which he spake unto them.

And he went down with them, and came to Nazareth, and was subject unto them: but his mother kept all these sayings in her heart.[84]

The King James Version (KJV) translation of "[She] kept all these sayings in her heart" does not reveal the full sense of the Greek text. A better translation might be, "[She] kept safe, or treasured up, all these sayings in her heart."[85]

A son's early years were certainly almost exclusively in the women's world. The bond between mother and son usually remained the strongest emotional tie throughout life. Thus, a young man's transition to the male, public world was often painful, difficult, and lengthy. Furthermore, in the traditional Mediterranean society, a wife did not look to her husband for companionship or comfort. That came from children and other women. This may explain Mary's feelings when she finds her son in the temple at Jerusalem. He seemingly has become independent of her world—and not only her world but of Joseph's also.

From age twelve to the start of his ministry, nothing is known about Jesus except that he "increased in wisdom and stature, and in favour with God and man," and, we must assume, so did Mary.[86] Her life during this period was assuredly centered around the home, but also around the synagogue. As we will see, Jesus was introduced to the synagogue in Nazareth as a young man, and his regular trip to this particular "house of prayer" continued until he began his ministry.

Mary's discipleship continued after her son's mission began. She was recorded as being present on several occasions through Jesus' three-year mission, and she faithfully reappears at the cross, as both a mother and a follower.

Chapter Seven

Once More Astonished:
Jesus' Parables and Women

$\mathcal{A}$s we have demonstrated, women played a significant role in stories recorded in the first chapters of the Gospels of Matthew and Luke. It is, therefore, not surprising that they also appeared in many of Jesus' parables, despite the fact that rabbinic parables pointedly avoided mentioning women.

Perhaps no other aspect of Jesus' teaching has received more attention than his parables, for they are the very key to understanding his mission to the last, least, and lost. Jewish society of this period was in many respects a typical ancient society. It consisted mostly of the poor and the very poor. Among the poor were also the powerless, notably women, children, and slaves. It is therefore not at all surprising that women figure prominently in some of Jesus' most profound parables.

The male characters in the parables are numerous and reflect the various positions men held during this period (bridegrooms, builders, doctors, fools, judges, kings, merchants, priests, publicans, poor men, rich men, servants, sons, stewards, thieves, and more). The female characters include bridesmaids (virgins), a woman searching for a lost coin, a widow seeking justice, and a handful of unspecified wives, mothers, and daughters mentioned in general terms.[1]

Most of these women's experiences speak of situations intimately familiar to them as part of the rhythms of their daily life: sewing patches, baking bread, making wine, sending for the doctor, serving meals, sweeping the house, watching children play in the market, and so on.[2]

Yet within the familiar household scene, the unexpected erupts. The patch tears the cloth, the wine bursts the skins, the action of yeast in the dough transforms the lump, the lamp is put under the bed, the master serves the meal to his servants, the friend calls at midnight.

It is possible to find beneath the surface of these stories a host of images and situations that are uniquely evocative of women's experience and speak deeply to them here and now.

The Widow and the Unjust Judge (Luke 18:1–8)

Luke provides us with a unique parable about an implacable widow and an unjust judge. The setting is Jesus teaching people about prayer. In Luke's Gospel, Jesus often addressed a single concern with two stories: one that had a man at the center and another that had a woman at the center of the story. One might expect that such parallelism was simply a teaching tool intended to reinforce a principle. However, it may also reveal Jesus' acute awareness that his audience consisted of both men and women.[3] In an attempt to make his message clearly understandable to both, he told two stories and encouraged both men and women to identify with the characters in the parables and apply the stories to themselves.

We find this male-female parallelism throughout Luke's record, not just in the pairing of parables. Men and women are both objects of the message and illustrations of God's dealing with his children. In this particular set of parables, an oppressed woman is the central character of the first story, and the second story focuses on a despised man—a tax or toll collector.[4]

In the first story, Jesus spoke of a poor widow in need of help. Since women normally did not appear in public courtrooms, we can assume that this widow has no male family member who can appear on her behalf. She is alone. In ancient society, this woman's behavior is not expected (her persistence would be viewed negatively). In fact, the Hebrew word for widow has the nuance of one who is silent, unable to speak.

Jesus used here the common form of reasoning from the lesser instance to the greater; that is, if the lesser case is true—that a widow can finally get through to an insensitive judge—how much more true is the greater case—that a petitioner will be heard by a sensitive God. The parable really focuses on the widow's struggle with the unjust judge, since her adversary plays no significant part in the story except as a necessary presupposition. The scene is likely an administrative court, not a religious court. If so, then we may assume that her adversary has already preceded her to court in order to bribe the judge. The judge is not righteous,[5] and therefore the widow's case seems hopeless since she has nothing to offer him. She does not want "vengeance" as the King James Version (KJV) suggests, but "vindication," or protection from her adversary.[6]

Her only asset is her persistence. The judge successfully resists her continual pleading for some time, but finally she begins to bother him. The judge fears that the woman might "weary" him and so grants her request.[7] Jesus then concluded the parable and began explaining it to the disciples, "Hear what the unjust judge saith."[8]

Like the widow, the disciples were alone in a world that oppressed and opposed them, but God's attitude was not like that of the unjust judge. If this wicked judge would vindicate this woman, how much more would God, who is good, vindicate his own elect.[9] Jesus indicated that the disciples' only hope of being vindicated is by being persistent in prayer at all times. To inspire them to this end, Jesus gave only the model of a destitute but resolute widow.

The Lost Coin (Luke 15:8–10)

The parables of the lost sheep and the lost coin in Luke are typical examples of a "twin similitude." Similar twin similitudes are found elsewhere in the synoptic Gospels; for example, the parables of the mustard seed and the leaven and the parables of the hidden treasure and the pearl.[10]

The story of the lost sheep concerns a man, that of the lost coin a woman (and perhaps they concern a rich man and a poor widow). In both, the figurative part begins with a rather lengthy question. They are separated from one another merely by the single conjunction "either." They have a similar content and almost the same application.

It is important to note that Jesus emphasized that the principle of the parables was more important than the gender of the person involved, for he used both a man and a woman to symbolize what he himself was doing among the "publicans and sinners."[11]

In the case of the lost coin, the woman might have been poor, making her diligent search for the silver coin certainly understandable. Jesus contrasted this poor woman with the preceding shepherd, who, with his one hundred sheep, would be considered rich. The loss of the coin represents a day's wages, a significant amount for the poor. She commences a thorough search of her dark, windowless, Jewish Palestinian home—therefore the lighting of a lamp is necessary. She looks carefully, leaving no corner uninspected until she finds the coin. "And when she hath found it, she calleth her friends and her neighbours together, saying, Rejoice with me; for I have found the piece which I had lost."[12]

Her reaction is one of pure joy—so joyous that she invites her female friends and neighbors (as the Greek text indicates) to a small celebration perhaps.[13] Of course, this reflected the social reality of first-century Jewish Palestine. A woman associated with other women, not mixed groups.

Jesus made his point by comparison, "*Likewise*, I say unto you, there is joy in the presence of the angels of God over one sinner that repenteth."[14] Jesus' choice of this poor housewife (a widow perhaps) demonstrated that women and their work were as valid as men and their activities in analogies describing Jesus' mission and the activity of his Father in finding the lost soul. It also reflected Jesus' concern to convey the good news in terms with which women could identify.

The Leaven (Matthew 13:33)

In another telling example Jesus showed that the kingdom of God would have inauspicious beginnings but an extraordinary fulfillment. The parable of the leaven, found in both Matthew and Luke, is comparable to that of the mustard seed.[15] One reflects the indoor labors of women and the other the outdoor activities of men.

"Another parable spake he unto them; The kingdom of heaven

is like unto leaven, which a woman took, and hid in three measures of meal, till the whole was leavened."[16]

Jesus employed the image of the leaven in a highly provocative way. In Passover observance, rabbinical Judaism considered leaven as a symbol of corruption, while unleaven stood for what was holy. The leaven therefore provided a surprising reversal of expectations as leaven represented the kingdom of God in Luke and the kingdom of heaven in Matthew.[17]

In drawing a positive parallel between this woman's work of making bread and his own work and mission, Jesus implied how much he valued such "woman's work," quite in contrast to the views of his surrounding culture.

The Unmerciful Servant (Matthew 18:23–35)

Rome was a slave society, a brutal system well attested to in Greco-Roman sources (as much as one-third of the population of largely Gentile urban areas were slaves). Slavery gave occasion for cruelty and sexual license. By Jesus' time, children of women in slavery had become the primary source for new slaves. The number of slaves increased in several other ways, however. First, as already noted, "exposed" children found alive were usually raised as slaves (female infants were the largest percentage of that number). Second, children, predominantly daughters, were often sold into slavery by their parents—Greek, Roman, and Jewish. Even in Jewish Palestine during the first century, having slaves was common.

Another form of slavery, debt-bondage, existed throughout the Greco-Roman world. In the parable of the unmerciful servant, Jesus gave a vivid picture of what might well happen to someone who defaulted on a debt to a member of the family of Herod or some other absentee landlord.

Enslavement of debtors was a widespread practice in Jewish Palestine at the time of Jesus. However, whether one was Jewish or Gentile made a difference in both the length of service (six years for a Jew and lifetime for Gentiles) and the types of humiliation experienced (a Jewish slave owned by another Jew was treated with some care). Harsh reality was often grimmer than rabbinic legislation though, as we know from Herod's order to sell people to foreigners.[18] In 40 B.C. Antigonus the Maccabean promised to give the Parthians one thousand talents and five hundred women in return for helping him to win the Jewish throne. To make up this large number of women, he had many Jewish women taken from their families.[19]

In his parable of the unmerciful servant, Jesus made mention of this particular social condition:

> Therefore is the kingdom of heaven likened unto a certain king, which would take account of his servants.
>
> And when he had begun to reckon, one was brought unto him, which owed him ten thousand talents.
>
> But forasmuch as he had not to pay, *his lord commanded him to be sold, and his wife, and children*, and all that he had, and payment to be made.
>
> The servant therefore fell down, and worshipped him, saying, Lord, have patience with me, and I will pay thee all.
>
> Then the lord of that servant was moved with compassion, and loosed him, and forgave him the debt.[20]

The servant (he is called *doulos* in Greek, which means "slave") owed his master an enormous sum of ten thousand talents and was very nearly sold with his wife and children; but he pleaded for mercy, and his master remitted the debt.[21] The servant subsequently put a fellow servant who owed him a mere one hundred denarii under guard (or in prison); but he himself ended up being delivered to "tormentors" until he cleared off his own debt to his lord.

The first servant, along with his wife and children, were originally condemned by the lord to be sold: this was permanent enslavement. The second servant had a temporary debt bondage imposed on him by a powerful member of the lord's household acting on his own authority. The first servant eventually suffered debt bondage, too, with torture thrown in.[22]

In the context of the social reality of first-century Greco-Roman and Jewish culture, this parable must have struck Jesus' listeners and later those who heard the Gospel text read to them as a significant criticism of an extremely vicious practice.

Jesus' teaching about the value of human life and dignity, in particular where women paid a heavier price, is part of the fulfillment of messianic scripture, as he himself noted. When Jesus entered the synagogue in Nazareth following his baptism, they "delivered unto him the book of the prophet Esaias [the New Testament form of Isaiah]":

> And when he had opened the book, he found the place where it was written,
> The Spirit of the Lord is upon me, because he hath anointed me to preach the gospel to the poor; he hath sent me to heal the brokenhearted, to preach deliverance to the captives, and recovering of sight to the blind, to set at liberty them that are bruised,
> To preach the acceptable year of the Lord.
> And he closed the book, and he gave it again to the minister, and sat down. And the eyes of all them that were in the synagogue were fastened on him.
> And he began to say unto them, This day is this scripture fulfilled in your ears.[23]

While it is certain that this prophecy has several levels of application (e.g., spiritual bondage and spirit world bondage), it nevertheless offers an insight to Jesus' view of debt bondage, slavery, and his prophetic mission to liberate those in prison, including the mothers, wives, and daughters who, by no fault of their own, were subjected to this cruel system.

A Woman in Travail (John 16:21)

In one of Jesus' most vivid metaphors describing the rewards of discipleship, he likened the joy of seeing him to the joy of a woman who underwent the travail of childbirth and then was delivered of a child: her joy knew no bounds. While in the Upper Room during the Last Supper, Jesus told the Twelve: "A woman when she is in travail hath sorrow, because her hour is come: but as soon as she is delivered of the child, she remembereth no more the anguish, for joy that a man is born into the world."[24]

Modern women often relate to the "sorrow, because her hour is come," but women anciently had another perspective. Childbirth was a very dangerous undertaking. Mothers frequently died while giving birth, and many newborns did not survive the ordeal either. There were no anesthetics to relieve pain and no effective medicines to protect the health of the mother and her new infant. Men lived an average of ten years longer than women, largely attributed to the fact that they were not subject to childbirth.

Jesus continued to his disciples reassuringly, "And ye now therefore have sorrow: but I will see you again, and your heart shall rejoice, and your joy no man taketh from you."[25]

The Wise and Foolish Virgins (Matthew 25:1–13)

Women anciently, as well as today, were very occupied with the rituals of feeding and feasting, which take on special significance at the celebration of births and marriages and in more solemn times of death and departure. The theme of celebration and feasting appears in several parables. The banquet image is, of course, a symbol of the coming kingdom of God at the end time. It is deeply embedded in the Hebrew scriptures (Old Testament) and intertestamental literature (the apocrypha and pseudepigrapha).[26]

Some scholars call Matthew 24–25 the Parousia discourse because Jesus here announced his Parousia—"a Greek word that is the technical term in the New Testament for the second coming of the Lord in glory to judge the world."[27] The parables of the wise and foolish virgins, the talents, and the last judgment are part of Jesus' last discourse.[28] With these three parables, Matthew brings the public ministry to an end; in the following chapter the passion narrative begins.[29] Matthew's contribution to the Gospel narratives is unique because only here do we have both the commendation of some women (the wise) and the condemnation of others (the foolish).

> Then shall the kingdom of heaven be likened unto ten virgins, which took their lamps, and went forth to meet the bridegroom.
> And five of them were wise, and five were foolish.
> They that were foolish took their lamps, and took no oil with them:
> But the wise took oil in their vessels with their lamps.
> While the bridegroom tarried, they all slumbered and slept.
> And at midnight there was a cry made, Behold, the bridegroom cometh; go ye out to meet him.

First-century Judean terra-cotta oil lamps

Then all those virgins arose, and trimmed their lamps.

And the foolish said unto the wise, Give us of your oil; for our lamps are gone out.

But the wise answered, saying, Not so; lest there be not enough for us and you: but go ye rather to them that sell, and buy for yourselves.

And while they went to buy, the bridegroom came; and they that were ready went in with him to the marriage: and the door was shut.

Afterward came also the other virgins, saying, Lord, Lord, open to us.

But he answered and said, Verily I say unto you, I know you not.

Watch therefore, for ye know neither the day nor the hour wherein the Son of man cometh.[30]

Some modern translations prefer to speak of "girls" or "bridesmaids," five of whom are "stupid" and five "clever" or "prudent" or "sensible." The traditional rendering was "foolish" and "wise" virgins. If women are envisioned equally with men as objects of God's grace, forgiveness, and blessings, then it is also true that Matthew 25 reveals that women are equally objects of God's judgment.

The story also emphasizes Jesus' insistence that women bear responsibility for their own salvation. Again, the paralleling stories about the talents dealing with men and this story dealing with women demonstrate Jesus' interest in having his message applicable to both men and women.[31]

Even in his prophecies regarding his second coming, Jesus used familiar images, including a woman's task of milling, to describe the events: "But as the days of Noe [the New Testament form of Noah] were, so shall also the coming of the Son of man be. . . . Then shall two be in the field; the one shall be taken, and the other left. Two women shall be grinding at the mill; the one shall be taken, and the other left. Watch therefore: for ye know not what hour your Lord doth come."[32]

By including the social concreteness of the two women at the mill, Jesus helped the women in his audience relate to his teaching. For many women, milling was a life-long task. Milling was done at night and required three hours of work to provide enough flour for a family of five or six. Whether a family had their own outdoor oven depended on their ability to provide fuel. Ordinary women arose in the morning to take their bread dough to a common village oven (accessed by females only), or less likely, to the village baker. Only the rich could afford to bake "clean" bread (not the "black" bread eaten by most peasants) or to purchase it from those who made it.

Two Debtors (Luke 7:36–50)

One day, Jesus was invited to the house of Simon the Pharisee assumedly for a festive banquet. All those reclining at the low dinner table would have been men. After partaking of the meal, Jesus told Simon a parable regarding two debtors.[33]

"And, behold, a woman in the city, which was a sinner, when she knew that Jesus sat at meat in the Pharisee's house, brought an alabaster box of ointment, and stood at his feet behind him weeping, and began to wash his feet with tears, and did wipe them with the hair of her head, and kissed his feet, and anointed them with the ointment."[34]

Life in Jewish Palestinian society typically allowed very little privacy. Everything honorable was expected to be done in public because only dishonorable people had something to hide. Thus, in villages the doors to houses were always open during the day (though a thin linen curtain often hung across to keep out the dust). This made it easy for the woman to find Jesus and enter Simon's home.

The woman was known for some misconduct; we are not told what she had done, only that she was a sinner. She brought a flask made of soft translucent stone with her, and, beginning to cry, she bathed Jesus' feet with her tears. She then apparently unbound her hair and began to dry his feet with it. Of course, this was unacceptable behavior for a woman—so much so that a man was not to recite the *Shema*, the Biblical prayer recited twice a day and placed in the *tefellin* (phylacteries) devices strapped to the arms and forehead of male members of the household and the *mezuzzah* (containers attached to the doorways of Jewish homes), in the presence of a woman whose hair was undone.[35]

According to one interpretation of the law of Moses, a man could divorce his wife for letting down her hair in the presence of another man.[36] However, that the woman's tears fell upon his feet and that she wiped them with her hair probably was unplanned and unanticipated even by her. She had probably entered the home to express her gratitude to Jesus, and the tears may have come unanticipated from the emotion of the moment. The woman then "kissed his feet, and anointed them with the ointment."[37]

"Now when the Pharisee which had bidden him saw it, he spake within himself, saying, This man, if he were a prophet, would have known who and what manner of woman this is that toucheth him: for she is a sinner."[38] Jesus answered Simon: "I have somewhat to say unto thee. And he saith, Master, say on." Jesus then continued with this parable: "There was a certain creditor which had two debtors: the one owed five hundred pence [five hundred days of wages for a common laborer], and the other fifty. And when they had nothing to pay, he frankly forgave them both. Tell me therefore, which of them will love him most? Simon answered and said, I suppose he, to whom he forgave most. And he said unto him, Thou hast rightly judged."[39]

Direct evidence of heavy indebtedness in first-century Jewish Palestine suggests that as much as 35 to 40 percent of the total agricultural production was extracted from small farmers in various assessments (tributes, tolls, and taxes). Peasant farmers unable to repay loans of seed or capital frequently became tenant share-croppers on their own land.

When Simon answered Jesus' question regarding which debtor would naturally show more gratitude, Jesus then applied the parable to Simon and the woman:

> Seest thou this woman? I entered into thine house, thou gavest me no water for my feet: but she hath washed my feet with tears, and wiped them with the hairs of her head.
>
> Thou gavest me no kiss: but this woman since the time I came in hath not ceased to kiss my feet.
>
> My head with oil thou didst not anoint: but this woman hath anointed my feet with ointment.
>
> Wherefore I say unto thee, Her sins, which are many, are forgiven; for she loved much: but to whom little is forgiven, the same loveth little.
>
> And he said unto her, Thy sins are forgiven.
>
> And they that sat at meat with him began to say within themselves, Who is this that forgiveth sins also?
>
> And he said to the woman, Thy faith hath saved thee; go in peace.[40]

The actions of women as characters in Jesus' parables emphasized the visibility Jesus gave them in a society where they were nearly invisible before the law, and in many cases also physically invisible behind a veil or a barrier in the synagogue.

Chapter Eight

Wives, Mothers, and Daughters:
Women in the Teaching of Jesus

The four Gospels contain many images of women but reveal very little about the larger fabric of their everyday lives. Images of women drawing water, grinding grain, anointing bodies, traveling, conversing, and praying hint at a widely diverse world of women's activity, but unfortunately do not provide a social context from which to make sense of those images as a larger whole.

The obvious disparity between men and women in Jesus' day, however, is a distinctive feature of antiquity. By and large, for the women in the Roman eastern empire (Greece, Asia Minor, Jewish Palestine, and Egypt), their clearly defined functions were (1) biological—to perpetuate the family by producing legitimate heirs, and (2) social, in that they looked after their households—the basis of society—and were required to do so with care and affection.

During his ministry, Jesus often said and did things that conflicted with Jewish attitudes and religious customs of his day, especially the interpretation of the Mosaic regulations as found in the oral law (identified as the "traditions of the elders [fathers]").

The oral law, also known as the oral Torah, defined what the written teachings (the five books of Moses known as the Torah: Genesis, Exodus, Leviticus, Numbers, and Deuteronomy) meant. Rabbinic Judaism maintained that when God revealed the Torah to Israel at Mount Sinai, the revelation was given in two media: the first in writing, as in the five books of Moses; the second orally, handed on through memorization and ultimately written down in the Mishnah and related writings.

The rabbis and sages who handed down these two forms of

the law believed that they were safeguarding the Torah from being unwittingly, carelessly, or unintentionally violated. The oral teachings were seen as a protective legislation that was as binding upon them as the written law itself.[1]

While Jesus was deeply concerned and committed to observe the intent of the law of God given to Moses (written Torah), he nevertheless questioned both the rabbinical interpretations and applications of the law and the written Torah itself. In this sense, Jesus stood apart from his contemporaries in that he did not stand *under* but rather *above* the written Torah that Moses received at Mount Sinai.

Jesus asked his contemporaries to either choose the "traditions of the elders [fathers]" or himself as the rightful revealer of God's word.[2] Many stories preserved in the four Gospels suggest that he deliberately forced each person to choose between the words of dead men who interpreted dead prophets, preserved on the skins of dead animals, or the living words that he personally brought to them.

Almost every story in the New Testament presents a situation in which Jesus purposely challenged his listeners' world view. Among these stories, there are many allusions to women and their place in society and at home.

When Jesus delivered the Sermon on the Mount, it certainly must have reminded Matthew of Moses, who ascended Mount Sinai to receive and then give the law of God to the ancient Israelites. Now Jesus revealed his law to their descendants on a mount. Although women are not directly addressed in this sermon, their situation nevertheless may be seen as included in Jesus' message.

Adultery (Matthew 5:27–28)

Of special relevance to women were the injunctions regarding adultery and divorce as he outlined the duty of each disciple.

> Ye have heard that it was said by them of old time, Thou shalt not commit adultery:
> But I say unto you, That whosoever looketh on a woman to lust after her hath committed adultery with her already in his heart.

And if thy right eye offend thee, pluck it out, and cast it from thee: for it is profitable for thee that one of thy members should perish, and not that thy whole body should be cast into hell.

And if thy right hand offend thee, cut it off, and cast it from thee: for it is profitable for thee that one of thy members should perish, and not that thy whole body should be cast into hell.[3]

The Joseph Smith Translation (JST) adds significantly to the passage: "But I say unto you, That whosoever looketh on a woman to lust after her hath committed adultery with her already in his heart. *Behold, I give unto you a commandment, that ye suffer none of these things to enter into your heart, for it is better that ye deny yourselves of these things, where in ye will take up your cross, than ye should be cast into hell.*"[4]

This is another instance in which Jesus identified the inward thought and desire that precede an act of sin. The seventh commandment, "Ye shall not commit adultery," and the tenth commandment, "Ye shall not covet your neighbour's wife," were referred to by Jesus with the phrase, "Ye have heard that it was said by them of old time."[5]

For Jesus, adultery involved not merely the physical act but also the desire for it. By eliminating the distinction between thought and action, this extension of the law of Moses against adultery suggested that no one should be regarded as a sex object. Unlike Jewish society at the time, where a man was largely seen as guiltless, being seduced by a wicked woman, the burden here was placed directly on the man. Again, Jesus completely dismissed the rabbinical suggestion that looking at a woman inevitably causes lust. He did not warn his followers against looking at a woman, but against doing so with lust. Women were to be recognized as individuals in their own right, as human beings, fellow disciples, not as objects of men's desires.

The phrase rendered in the KJV as "hath committed adultery with her" could be read to mean "he commits adultery against her." The case is that of a man who looks with lust upon a woman who may not even know that she is being visually "undressed" by the man. He "adulterates her." The guilty man treats the woman as an adulteress, but this does not mean that she is actually that. He has made her that in his own mind.

It appears that at the time, contemporary Jews saw the act of adultery and coveting a neighbor's wife as an act against the father's or husband's property rights rather than against the woman herself. Sexual relations between an Israelite man, albeit married, and an unmarried or unbetrothed woman was not considered by rabbinical tradition to be adultery. It is therefore significant that Jesus does not speak of someone else's wife here, but simply of a woman in general. To treat any woman as a sex object and not as a person in her own right is sinful; all the more so when that woman is one's own wife.

Divorce (Matthew 5:31–32; 19:3–9; Mark 10:2–12; Luke 16:18)

Jesus continued to provide the new law of God—a radical challenge to Mosaic authority and the law itself: "It hath been said, Whosoever shall put away his wife, let him give her a writing of divorcement: But I say unto you, That whosoever shall put away his wife, saving for the cause of fornication, causeth her to commit adultery: and whosoever shall marry her that is divorced committeth adultery."[6]

This of course counters the Mosaic provisions of Deuteronomy and bypasses scribal disputes over the proper grounds for divorce.[7] Jesus insists that the Mosaic ruling concerning divorce was a temporary concession to human weakness. Men could divorce a wife for three main justifications, according to one interpretation of the law of Moses (that of Hillel—ca. 50 B.C. to ca. A.D. 10).[8] First, sexual misconduct; second, "even if she spoiled a dish for him"; and finally, "even if he found another fairer than she."[9] The double standard reflects the low social status of women.

To be sure, the law of Moses did not command divorce, and both the Old Testament and rabbinic tradition view it with some distaste.[10] Nevertheless, since the law outlines the proper procedures for divorce, it was natural to conclude that Moses sanctioned divorce. Jesus, therefore, was perceived as challenging both Mosaic authority and current Jewish practice.

Among the Essene community, in spite of their literal interpretation of the Torah, the Qumran people came to maintain a view of marriage and a practice of marriage radically different from that contained in both the Hebrew scriptures and rabbinical literature of the period. Not all Essenes practiced celebacy: young men had the right to take a wife and live with her for five years. After this period, the laws stipulated that he was to refrain entirely from sexual cohabitation with his wife. If she died before the five-year period ended, he could not take another wife, for he had already done his duty in "replenishing the earth." The man was not forced to divorce his wife after five years, but it was likely that such divorces occurred. According to their own writings, once a man reached the age of twenty-five he was to live in sexual abstinence in order to be able to do his part in the holy war against the "children of darkness."[11]

Against a backdrop of various interpretations and practices concerning divorce in his day, Jesus, in another setting, attempted to reestablish the relationship between woman and man as it existed between Adam and Eve before the Fall.[12] The Pharisees were acting as hostile questioners regarding a law of the Torah: Notice that every time Jesus' opponents put a hostile question to him, he answers with a counterquestion. Jesus distances himself from their interpretation of Moses with an emphasis on the word *you:*

> And the Pharisees came to him, and asked him, Is it lawful for a man to put away his wife? tempting him.
> And he answered and said unto them, What did Moses command you?
> And they said, Moses suffered to write a bill of divorcement, and to put her away.
> And Jesus answered and said unto them, For the hardness of your heart he wrote you this precept.
> But from the beginning of the creation God made them male and female.
> For this cause shall a man leave his father and mother, and cleave to his wife;
> And they twain shall be one flesh: so then they are no more twain, but one flesh.
> What therefore God hath joined together, let not man put asunder.[13]

The married couple were "no more twain, but one flesh." This indicates a biological or blood relationship rather than a legal one. Because it is a biological relationship, like the relationship to mother and father or to one's brothers and sisters or children, marriage cannot be legally dissolved.

The disciples themselves seemed shocked by his response and questioned him in private: "And in the house his disciples asked him again of the same matter. And he saith unto them, Whosoever shall put away his wife, and marry another, committeth adultery against her. And if a woman shall put away her husband, and be married to another, she committeth adultery."[14]

A careful reading of the text shows that Jesus took a remarkable position in light of the social reality of his day. First, he taught that divorce was not necessarily prohibited, but divorce and remarriage or divorce in order to marry again was. Jesus also acknowledged the right of women to divorce.

Most astonishing was that Jesus taught that if a man married again, he would commit adultery. Given first-century Jewish interpretation, a man could not commit adultery in such a case. Adultery against whom? Against his wife it seems. Finally, Jesus championed the rights of a faithful wife and her right *not* to be divorced.

A literal translation of the Greek text seems to indicate that any innocent woman who was divorced was "made adulterous," that is, she was treated as though she were an adulteress. She was victimized in being cast out, even as an adulteress wife was cast out. The bill of divorce distinguished her from a real adulteress, but Jesus gave no real value to this distinction. He stressed what the innocent wife and the guilty wife shared in common—both were cast out.

Jesus taught that an innocent wife's rights were to be retained and respected. Her rights were not being preserved by the bill of divorce that her husband gave her. He had in fact degraded her and exposed her to continuing injustice.

Honor Your Father and Mother (Mark 7:9–13; Matthew 15:3–6)

In Mark and parallel accounts, Jesus affirmed the Mosaic commandment of honoring one's parents. Jesus, with more than a little anger and irony, charged religious leaders with "making the word of God of none effect through your tradition."[15] It is certain that the fifth commandment was originally addressed to adults. It was a prescription requiring the able-bodied children to care for and support the elderly members of the extended family.

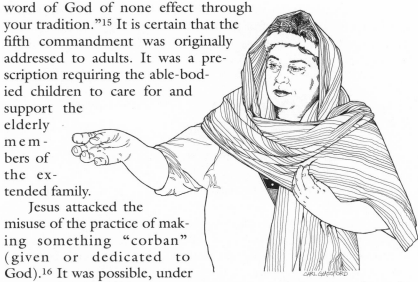

Jesus attacked the misuse of the practice of making something "corban" (given or dedicated to God).[16] It was possible, under rabbinic ruling, to declare in a vow, using the term *corban,* that one's parents were forbidden to benefit from one's property because that property was dedicated to another purpose, primarily the temple.

First, Jesus reminded his listeners that Moses taught the Israelites to revere both father and mother. This is significant since some rabbis taught that one should honor father more than mother. Next, Jesus reasserted the negative enjoinder of Moses: "Whoso curseth father or mother, let him die the death."[17]

It is hard to imagine a more strongly worded way of enforcing children's obligations to parents and, especially in this case, to dependent parents. Under one interpretation of the law, what had originally been intended as a means to set aside property or even oneself for the purpose of God became a means of preventing others from having a claim on one's property. Sometimes this vow may have been made in a moment of anger and thus might have involved some hint of a curse. If such was the case, this may explain why Jesus referred to the commandment against cursing or speaking evil of one's parents.

According to Jesus, some rabbis, because of their traditions, had allowed one's duty to fulfill a vow to take precedence over (and in effect nullify) the duty to honor one's parents. Thus Jesus affirmed the moral obligation of a child to provide for his aging or indigent parents; both mother and father were to be honored in word and deed. The Greek word *timao* (honor), chosen by Mark to represent Jesus' meaning, implies, in the case of aged parents, support and help.[18]

Little Children (Mark 9:33–37; Matthew 18:1–5; Luke 9:46–48)

As already noted, even during the first century A.D., exposure of infants (especially girls) was widely practiced in Greco-Roman society. In an otherwise sensitive letter of a Roman soldier stationed in Egypt in 1 B.C. to his wife in Italy, we read: "If by chance you bear a child, if it is a boy, let it be, if it is a girl, expose it."[19]

Ancient attitudes towards children are singularly paradoxical. Parents undoubtedly loved their children, yet the treatment accorded children was often severe, even brutal. It was not uncommon for children to begin working at five years of age, especially children of slaves or ordinary farm families. Their work began at sunrise and concluded at sunset. The transition from childhood to the adult world of work came abruptly.[20]

Children were valued highly in Judaism; nonetheless, sons were valued more highly than daughters, even among Jews. There is no evidence that children, either male or female, were considered as religious models by the rabbis, for in rabbinic Judaism it was the wise and learned rabbi, not the child, who was an example to disciples wishing to be great in the kingdom of heaven. Jesus' positive attitude towards children contrasted sharply with common attitudes of that era:[21]

> And he came to Capernaum: and being in the house he asked them, What was it that ye disputed among yourselves by the way?
>
> But they held their peace: for by the way they had disputed among themselves, who should be the greatest.
>
> And he sat down, and called the twelve, and saith unto them, If any man desire to be first, the same shall be last of all, and servant of all.
>
> And he took a child [*paidion*], and set [it] in the midst of them: and when he had taken [it] in his arms, he said unto them,
>
> Whosoever shall receive one of such children in my name, receiveth me: and whosoever shall receive me, receiveth not me, but him that sent me.[22] [The term *paidion* (child) is neuter, so it cannot

be known whether Jesus selected a little boy or a little girl to make his point.[23]]

Rather remarkable was Jesus' assertion that whoever received a child welcomed Jesus. The verb translated "receive" is often used to refer to hospitality, the welcoming of a guest.[24] Perhaps Jesus identified himself with the helpless so that they would be helped by those who wished to serve him. This story is followed in the next chapter of Mark by an account of several individuals who brought their children to Jesus so he could bless them.

Blessing Children (Mark 10:13–16; Matthew 19:13–15; Luke 18:15–17)

Several parents, and perhaps older children, brought younger children to Jesus so he might touch them. Perhaps reflecting the typical attitude that children were less mature and thus less important than adults, the disciples rebuked those who were bringing the children forward.[25] Luke changed Mark's word for "children" to "infants"; possibly both were present.[26] The setting is likely that of peasant women, many of whose babies would be dead within a year of birth, fearfully holding those babies out for Jesus to touch and bless.

Jesus reacted to the disciples' rebuke with displeasure: "Suffer [allow] the little children to come unto me, and forbid them not: for of such is the kingdom of God."[27] In the context of Mark 10, the contrast between the ease with which children enter the kingdom and the difficulty with which the rich enter is notable.[28] Jesus' positive attitude about children, their place in the kingdom, and how they might serve as models for disciples and be served by disciples implies a positive estimation of the woman's role as mother and childbearer, the father's role as provider and caregiver, and the child's role as innocent learner.

Lot's Wife (Luke 17:32)

In the middle of a discourse dealing with his second coming, Jesus said, "Remember Lot's wife."[29] The entire speech dealt with the need for readiness in the day when the kingdom of God would come to earth. These same sayings are almost all found (somewhat differently arranged) in Matthew 24. In Luke, however, Jesus added to the example of Noah, that of Lot's wife (again the double pairing that makes the discourse gender inclusive). In giving this proverb, "Remember Lot's wife," Jesus warned those present about neglecting the signs of the times—it is fatal to look back once you have begun your journey to discipleship.

This addition, one of the rare times that a woman is used as a negative example in the four Gospels, reminds us that Jesus saw women as responsible for their own actions and therefore free to choose actions that would either reserve or deny them a place in his kingdom.

A Widow of Sidon (Luke 4:25–26)

Jesus' own experience in Nazareth was foreshadowed by the Old Testament prophet Elijah: "But I tell you of a truth, many widows were in Israel in the days of Elias [the New Testament form of Elijah], when the heaven was shut up three years and six months, when great famine was throughout all the land; But unto none of them was Elias sent, save unto Sarepta [the New Testament form of Zarephath], a city of Sidon, unto a woman that was a widow."[30]

The widow lived in a Phoenician town on the Mediterranean coast between Tyre and Sidon and was a Gentile, not a Jew. The use of a Gentile widow (along with pairing this story with that of the Gentile man, Naaman, mentioned in the following verse) may also prefigure the expansion of the gospel beyond Judaism.

The Queen of the South (Matthew 12:42)

Paralleling a saying concerning the men of Nineveh, Jesus said, "The queen of the south shall rise up in the judgment with this generation, and shall condemn it: for she came from the uttermost parts of the earth to hear the wisdom of Solomon; and, behold, a greater than Solomon is here."[31] She is probably the queen of Sheba mentioned in the Old Testament.[32]

Jesus reasoned that if a Gentile, "the queen of the south," sought Solomon for wisdom in ancient days, then the Jews should seek wisdom from "a greater than Solomon," meaning himself. Again Jesus implied that a Gentile woman often was more discernable than male Jewish leaders. Also, like the Ninevites, she is a Gentile who will receive a more favorable final judgment than the Jews.

Gathering in His Name (Matthew 18:20)

Women were not counted in a *minyan* (the quorum of ten required for public prayer)—they were classified with children and slaves, who similarly did not qualify as part of the number necessary.

Jesus may have had this in mind when he told his disciples, "For where two or three are gathered in my name, there am I in the midst of them."[33] He did not differentiate between men and women, and of course also rejected the rabbinical idea that ten men were needed to worship.

Those That Hear and Keep It (Luke 11:27–28)

As already noted, women in Israel were honored for their motherhood. Both husband and wife prayed for sons and celebrated when they were born and again when they were circumcised and given a name at eight days. No corresponding observance marked the birth of a daughter, however. "The world cannot exist without males and females," a rabbinical saying states, "But happy is he whose children are sons and woe to him whose children are daughters."[34] The rabbi always gave this blessing to a newly wed couple, "[The Lord] bless thee and guard [keep] thee; . . . bless thee [with] sons, and guard [keep] thee [from] daughters."[35] A woman with daughters but without sons was considered childless by many of Jesus' contemporaries.

Jesus took an opportunity to respond to such ideas when a woman in a crowd spoke up: "Blessed is the womb that bare thee, and the paps which thou hast sucked."[36] Her statement implies an understanding of how a woman may be accounted blessed—

through being a mother to a great son. Jesus responded, "Yea rather, blessed are they that hear the word of God and keep it."[37]

Obviously, for Jesus it was much more important to hear God's word and observe it than it was to give birth to a great rabbi or even the Messiah himself. For this reason, Mary was blessed—not because of her functional, biological role, but because she heard the word and chose to obey it.[38]

A Woman Married Seven Times (Matthew 22:23–33; Mark 12:18–27; Luke 20:27–40)

Based on the law of Moses, Jews often participated in levirate marriages (from *levir*, Latin for brother-in-law).[39] Such marriages were imposed on close male relatives as a duty since a childless widow had the right to have her dead husband's name continue.

The Sadducees, who denied the resurrection of the dead, took the opportunity to confront Jesus with a technical discussion of the law in relation to the resurrection. Obviously, the Sadducees' inquiry was not an innocent quest for theological clarification but rather an attempt to force Jesus to either repudiate the Mosaic commandment or prove the absurdity of the belief in resurrection.

> The same day came to him the Sadducees, which say that there is no resurrection, and asked him,
>
> Saying, Master, Moses said, If a man die, having no children [the Hebrew text says "son"], his brother shall marry his wife, and raise up seed unto his brother.
>
> Now there were with us seven brethren: and the first, when he had married a wife, deceased, and, having no issue, left his wife unto his brother:
>
> Likewise the second also, and the third, unto the seventh.
>
> And last of all the woman died also.
>
> Therefore in the resurrection whose wife shall she be of the seven? for they all had her.[40]

The story demonstrates the Sadducees' inability to view the woman's situation in any other way than through their own male-centered categories. It never crossed their minds that a woman had a choice in the matter. Whatever the doctrinal implications marriages performed under the law of Moses (without sealing keys) may have is not our interest here. For us, the story reveals Jewish leaders' attitudes of the day towards women.

Pregnant and Nursing Mothers (Mark 13:17; Matthew 24:19; Luke 21:23)

Known as the "little apocalypse," Mark 13 described two catastrophic events: one to occur in the first century and another at the "end" of time as foretold by Jesus.[41] "And as he went out of the temple, one of his disciples saith unto him, Master, see what manner of stones and what buildings are here! And Jesus answering said unto him, Seest thou these great buildings? there shall not be left one stone upon another, that shall not be thrown down."[42]

In describing the one that his generation would experience, presumably the destruction of Jerusalem in A.D. 70, Jesus showed special compassion for women, especially those pregnant and nursing mothers who would have to flee their homes in those days. "But woe to them that are with child, and to them that give suck in those days!"[43] The immediate subject had to do with the fate of the nation and its great city and temple, but Jesus was not forgetful of those for whom it would have special sufferings, including those carrying unborn babies and those nursing babies.

Jesus' striking teachings and attitudes regarding women were lived out in his day-to-day life as he met them along the way, as we will see in the remaining chapters.

Chapter Nine

Along the Way:
The Women Jesus Met

$\mathcal{A}$s we have noted, Jesus often told stories relating to women's activities. He spoke of patching worn-out clothes, grinding wheat, making bread, and cleaning homes. He spoke of daughters, wives, mothers, and widows. He used examples of women to portray gospel principles and practices. Jesus taught that women were not of only secondary significance, but rather that they were an integral part of the divine creation, both necessary and significant, having worth as individuals in their own right and not simply in relation to their fathers or husbands.

Following Jesus' death, the Twelve proclaimed the gospel and often told crowds of his mortal ministry, of "how God anointed Jesus of Nazareth with the Holy Ghost and with power: who went about *doing good.*"[1]

This "doing good" is more specifically defined as healing the sick and casting out devils. All four Gospels agree that Jesus showed compassion for the sick and those who were possessed by the devil, some of the prisoners whom the Messiah was to set free.[2] Among the prisoners who were physically, emotionally, or spiritually incarcerated were many women. The stories in this chapter prove that Jesus fulfilled the commission he announced in Nazareth to preach the good news to the poor and proclaim release to the captives and oppressed—both men and women.

He came as an unknown into a village of lower Galilee to preach in their synagogue.[3] The people of the village watched him carefully through callous, hard eyes, having lived long enough at subsistence level to know exactly where the line was drawn between poverty and destitution. They were among the nearly three-quarters of a million inhabitants of Jewish Palestine, most of whom lived in similar conditions.[4] Their life was based on a barter economy and they worked hard in agriculture and small workshops without being able to protect themselves from oppressive absentee landlords and corrupt political and military personnel representing the power of Rome or their client kings and rulers.

The man from Nazareth probably looked just like them, a poor Jewish peasant, as he spoke about the kingdom of heaven with "authority, not as the scribes."[5] These people knew all about kingdoms and empires, rule and power, but they knew it in terms of heavy taxes, rents, tolls, mounting debt, malnutrition, sickness, disease, and emotional and physical captivity to forces that were beyond their control and apparently their understanding.

What these people, many of whom were women, wanted to really know is what could this kingdom Jesus proclaimed do for a sick child, a blind spouse, a maimed parent, or an insane soul screaming in agonizing isolation?

In his first miracle among those he met along the way, Jesus rebuked an unclean spirit from a desperate and demented soul. Now the villagers listened once more, but now with curiosity giving way to embarrassment for their lack of faith: "And they were all amazed, insomuch that they questioned among themselves, saying, What thing is this? what new doctrine is this? for with authority commandeth he even the unclean spirits, and they do obey him."[6]

To those first disciples who asked how to repay him for his intervention, Jesus gave a simple answer—simple, that is, to understand, but hard to undertake. You are healed healers, he said, so take the kingdom to others.[7] It is, was, and always will be available to any who want it—women and men alike.

The Widow of Nain (Luke 7:11–17)

Jesus and his disciples came to a "city called Nain," located at the northern foot of Mount Moreh in the eastern Jezreel Valley of Galilee.[8] It was a rigorous march uphill from Capernaum, about twenty-five miles away.[9] While nearing the gate, "behold, there was a dead man carried out, the only son of his mother, and she was a widow: and much people of the city was with her. And when the Lord saw her, he had compassion on her, and said unto her, Weep not. And he came and touched the bier: and they that bare him stood still. And he said, Young man, I say unto thee, Arise. And he that was dead sat up, and began to speak. And he delivered him to his mother."[10]

This story is somewhat different from many other miracle stories in that it is solely Jesus' compassion which motivates his actions. In many other instances, the faith of the recipient is an important element.[11] Why Jesus has compassion on this woman is perhaps explained by the phrase, "the only son of his mother, and she was a widow."[12] It stresses the dire circumstances the woman found herself in (no legal male protector and no one to support her in her advancing years)—a situation that drove many women into complete destitution, poverty, and often an early death.

More than one-half of all families were broken during the childbearing and child-rearing years by the death of one or both parents. Thus, widows and orphans were everywhere. Since in death her son could not marry, the woman faced the end of the family line, the loss of its land (if they had any), and hence the loss of the family's place in the village.

According to rabbinical Judaism, "Four are regarded dead: the leper, the blind, he who is childless, and he who has become impoverished. He who is childless is learned from Rachel; Or else I am dead."[13] The compassion of Jesus for both mother and son is manifested by his willingness to "touch" the bier, thus making himself ritually unclean in order to *restore* the son's life and to *restore* the son to his mother.

The Woman Taken in Adultery (John 8:1–11)

This beautiful and poignant story could be called, "Scribes, Pharisees, and a Woman," since it really focuses on each. The first scene of the story is quite dramatic. Jesus entered the temple to teach: "Early in the morning [literally—at daybreak] he came again into the temple, and all the people came unto him; and he sat down, and taught them. And the scribes and Pharisees brought unto him a woman taken in adultery; and when they had set her in the midst, They say unto him, Master, this woman was taken in adultery, in the very act."[14]

This story reveals much about how some women were treated and viewed in Jewish Palestine at the time. According to the law of Moses, a man who had the "spirit of jealousy of his wife," that is, he suspected that she had committed adultery, brought her to the temple to undergo a test or an ordeal to prove her innocence or guilt.[15]

If she admitted to the act, there were witnesses, or she refused to participate in the test, she was not required to undergo the ordeal. The result—she was immediately divorced and forced to relinquish her dowry, the only economic protection she had. However, if she maintained her innocence she was forced to submit to the test of bitter water.

In the temple, "before the Lord"—that is, before the altar— she was obligated to drink a potentially poisonous draught composed largely of water, dirt from the temple floor, and the ink scratched from a parchment containing a curse—hence the name "bitter water."[16] The drink would supposedly have no effect if she was innocent. If she was guilty, however, her belly would swell and her thigh rot.[17] The bitter water test was only administered to women, not to men, since only a man could accuse his spouse of adultery, not vice versa.

As was the case with many Mosaic dictums, additional layers were added. Our sources, dating from before A.D. 70, outline the procedure practiced at the time of Jesus. The woman was brought to the Court of Women the same place where Jesus met the woman in this story.[18] The priest seized her garments and tore them down to the waist so as to expose her breasts, unlike the Mosaic commandment of simply uncovering her head.[19]

The additional humiliation of uncovering the breasts of the suspected (not just the convicted) adulteress was intended to motivate her voluntary confession if she was guilty and to discourage her from resorting to the ordeal.

The priest then unloosened her hair (most women wore their hair in a long braid). All jewelry was removed and she was bound tight (around the breasts) with a cord. This rope was known as an Egyptian cord, because she was accused of following the immoral practices of Egypt.

Anyone could examine her at this point, except her own slaves if she had any. Some rabbis believed that all the women in the Court of Women at the time were *required* to look at her as some type of object lesson. After this degrading experience, the priest offered her the bitter water drink already mentioned and waited for the sign.

If this shameful act could be carried out at a husband's minor suspicion based on the flimsiest of evidence, what actions took place against a woman "caught in the very act," as our story suggests? We know that part of an adulteress's punishment was to strip off her clothes.[20] We do not know at what point in the women's judgment this action was taken, only that it was. We are left only to imagine the traumatic situation this woman found herself in among these men (and whoever else was present).

When the scribes and Pharisees brought the woman to Jesus, they dehumanized her, turning her into an object for debate and discussion. The woman was caught in the very act of intercourse. According to the book of Deuteronomy, there must be at least two witnesses of the action, exclusive of the husband.[21]

She must have been a married woman since only the unfaithful conduct of a wife was a concern of rabbinic attention, not affairs between husbands and unmarried women. It is not beyond reason that the woman had been set up by her estranged husband, who had witnesses ready and waiting. One may ask, if she was caught "in the very act," where was the man? This demonstrates the prevailing double standard.

The men asked Jesus to judge her case: "Now Moses in the law commanded us, that such should be stoned: but what sayest thou? This they said, tempting him, that they might have to accuse him."[22] Actually, the Mosaic law does order the death penalty, but leaves the manner of causing death unspecified.[23] Since the Romans had recently taken away from the Sanhedrin the right of imposing capital punishment(A.D. 30), it seems clear why the woman was brought to Jesus. If he decided that the woman should be punished according to the Mosaic law, he would be in trouble with the civil authorities; if he decided the case in favor of the woman and released her, he would violate the clear prescriptions of the word of God.[24] John is precise about their underlying motives, "This they said, *tempting him*, that they might have to accuse him."

Jesus then bent down and wrote on the ground with his finger "as though he heard them not."[25] The scribes and Pharisees continued to press him for an answer, so Jesus stood and addressed them directly, "He that is without sin among you, let him first cast a stone at her."[26] In the Mosaic law, the witnesses against the accused have a special responsibility for her death.[27]

It would be an error to see in this instance an argument that a judge must be sinless in order to judge others and execute justice according to his responsibilities. The men here may have been zealous for the law, but they did not appear to be interested in the *purpose* of the law, the spiritual state of the woman, or her penitent condition (these issues never entered the discussion). Moreover, Jesus knew that they were merely using her as a pawn to entrap him. Jesus questioned the corrupt motives of the scribes and Pharisees (the judges in the story), the witnesses, and the husband of the wife. By his act, Jesus also repudiated the double standard of bringing the woman forward but not her male lover.

When Jesus finished saying these things to the men, "again he stooped down, and wrote on the ground."[28] These are the only references in the scriptures that Jesus wrote anything. There has been some speculation as to what he may have written in the dust. Some early manuscript versions of John added "the sins of every one of them," but this was probably just an attempt by early copyists to satisfy such curiosity.[29]

When the crowd heard him, they began to leave, "convicted by their own conscience." Eventually everyone left except the woman "standing in the midst."[30] At this moment, the sinful daughter of Abraham stood confronted with the sinless Son of God.

Jesus stood up again and spoke to the woman twice: "When Jesus had lifted up himself, and saw none but the woman, he said unto her, Woman, where are those thine accusers? hath no man condemned thee? She said, No man, Lord. And Jesus said unto her, Neither do I condemn thee: go, and sin no more."[31] John demonstrates through this story the delicate balance between Jesus' justice in not condoning the sin and his mercy in forgiving the sinner.

One of the most striking features of this story is that Jesus, unlike the scribes and Pharisees, treated this woman as the equal of her accusers. Jesus asked them to focus on the past, "He who is without sin among you, let him first cast a stone at her," and he asked the woman to focus on the future, "Go, and sin no more." Jesus invited both the woman and the men to begin life anew.

They were invited to give up old ways and enter a new way of life through him, since they all were in need of repentance. Mercy was offered to both groups, but only the woman took advantage of the offer. The Joseph Smith Translation (JST) adds, "And the woman glorified God from that hour, and believed on his name."[32]

On another occasion, Jesus clarified his mission to all Israel. To the "chief priests and the elders of the people," Jesus proclaimed that members of the two most despised groups in Jewish Palestine—tax collectors (in all likelihood toll agents of the occupying Roman government or local kings and rulers) and prostitutes (one of the lowest, if not the lowest, social groups in Jewish society)—accept the message of repentance and redemption. This group lived outside the city walls of Jerusalem with beggars, persons in undesirable occupations, and landless peasants who drifted toward the city in search of day-laboring opportunities. He reminded them, "For John came unto you in the way of righteousness, and ye believed him not: but the publicans and the harlots believed him, and ye, when ye had seen it, repented not afterward, that ye might believe."[33]

This story reminds us of another event recorded in Mark. "Jesus withdrew himself with his disciples to the sea and a great multitude from Galilee followed him, and from Judaea, and from Jerusalem, and from Idumaea, and from beyond Jordan; and they about Tyre and Sidon."[34]

Like the publicans and harlots who went out to listen to John, large groups of people traveled long distances to hear Jesus preach. Those from Idumaea, for example, had walked some one hundred and fifty miles to the Sea of Galilee. Following Jesus was not always convenient; it not only meant giving up time, but in many cases, it meant traveling long distances, often by foot, to walk with him.

The Woman Healed on the Sabbath (Luke 13:10–17)

The Jewish Sabbath, the seventh and last day of the week, like all other days, begins at sundown rather than sunrise. The general requirement to keep it as a day of rest is one of the Ten Commandments.[35] Mosaic regulations prescribe death by stoning as the punishment for deliberate transgression.[36] Unwitting or inadvertent transgression required a sin offering at the temple.[37]

Certainly, Sabbath observance was one of the most unusual aspects of standard Jewish practice. Even non-Jews recognized this. The Sabbath day was an occasion for special sacrifices in the temple and for prayer and study in the synagogue.

All our sources, including the four Gospels, are unanimous with regard to the strictness of Jewish Sabbath observance. However, some groups, including the Pharisees, debated certain aspects of Sabbath observance. They modified the Sabbath law in various ways, in many cases making it stricter. For example, they believed healing on the Sabbath was a breach of law, except in dire circumstances when someone's life was threatened. Some rabbis also believed that healing in the "house of prayer"—the synagogue—was also not appropriate.[38]

Luke recorded an instance in which Jesus healed a woman on the Sabbath, which of course drew the attention of those who saw it. Our story begins when Jesus saw a woman who was doubled up with paralysis: "And he was teaching in one of the synagogues on the sabbath. And, behold, there was a woman which had a spirit of infirmity eighteen years, and was bowed together, and could in no wise lift up herself. And when Jesus saw her, he called her to him, and said unto her, Woman, thou art loosed from thine infirmity. And he laid his hands on her: and immediately she was made straight, and glorified God."[39]

She was not simply a faithful woman bent over with arthritis, as she is usually portrayed. Luke uses the same verb, *anakupto,* "raise oneself up," or "look up" as he does in the sentence, "*look up,* and lift up your heads, for your redemption draweth nigh."[40] It may have its parallel in the saying about "weak hands and the feeble knees," which are to be lifted up with the hope of the Messiah.[41] The fact that she could not look up also meant that she had no hope; she could not raise her head and see Jesus' redemptive approach.

After the woman is healed, "the ruler of the synagogue answered with indignation, because that Jesus had healed on the sabbath day, and said unto the people, There are six days in which men ought to work: in them therefore come and be healed, and not on the sabbath day."[42]

Jesus countered the criticism for not waiting until the next day to heal the woman, "Ought not this woman, being a daughter of Abraham . . . be loosed from this bond on the sabbath day?"[43]

Thus, he declares the Sabbath to be the day for healing *par excellence:* the Sabbath is not to prohibit works of compassion but to encourage them.

Jesus' description of the woman as "a daughter of Abraham" is unique. Previously Jews have been called the children of Abraham or a son of Abraham, but never a daughter. Here Jesus placed in context all who come under the covenant, all being deserving of divine favor and blessings.

The Poor Widow (Mark 12:41–44; Luke 21:1–4)

When Jesus entered the temple in Jerusalem during his last week, he encountered a woman. At the end of a long day of teaching and discussion, just before telling his disciples about the signs of the end of the world, Jesus watched a poor widow throw two coins into the temple treasury in the Court of Women.[44] Women and men were allowed in this area of the temple, but women could not proceed any further into the holy sanctuary. As many as thirteen trumpet-shaped receptacles were located here to receive the donations.

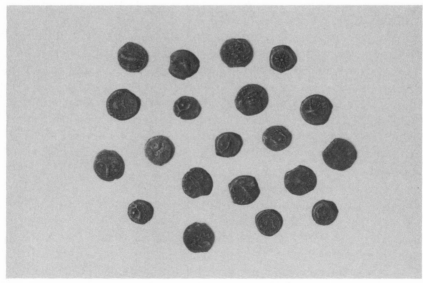

Judean leptons ("widow's mites"), the smallest coins in circulation in first-century Jewish Palestine

The people who worshiped at the temple donated a free-will offering into the treasury. While many cast in much, Jesus noticed in particular this widow casting in two leptons—"mites" as the King James Version calls them, the smallest coins in circulation in Jewish Palestine. The lepton was a tiny Hebrew bronze coin equivalent to 1/128th of a denarius (about a quarter to half a cent), and two were not even enough to feed oneself a simple meal.

Jesus "called unto him his disciples, and saith unto them, Verily I say unto you, That this poor widow hath cast more in than all they which have cast into the treasury: For all they did cast in of their abundance; but she of her want did cast in all that she had, even all her living."[45]

While not all widows were poor, most lived a precarious existence since their major source of protection and identity, their husband, was dead. While sons, other male relatives, or family wealth could provide a measure of security, widows were traditionally considered subjects of special moral concern because of their generally defenseless legal and financial position in ancient society.[46] In the scene immediately before this story, Jesus condemned the scribes for, among other things, consuming the homes of widows.[47] This was probably accomplished by appointing some well-known and pious man as the executor of the estate of the dead husband, only to have him use the resources for his own advantage and thus "devour" the widow's house.

A widow was not only disadvantaged by poverty but also by her vulnerable status as an unmarried woman, thus rendering her practically invisible in the legal, political, social, and religious eyes of first-century Jewish society.

This particular widow's dire situation is demonstrated by the fact that she cast "all that she had" into the treasury—"two mites." Most of those who were poor, who did not know where they would get food to still their hunger, who cried and heard the cries of their children, were women (widows) and the fatherless children dependent on them.

The New Testament contrasts the gifts of the crowd and the widow with two interesting Greek words.[48] The term translated in the King James Version as "want" is associated with "not enough," technically her total means of subsistence; while the other term, "abundance," is opposed to the first and reflects the notion of "more than enough" or "extremely rich." What Jesus says about her offering is that it is greater than those who gave of their abundance since it is the nature of the act of giving that matters to God rather than the gross amount one may give.

Two Stories—One Purpose (Mark 5:22–43; Matthew 9:18–26; Luke 8:41–56)

Every ancient culture had its anxiety about touching. In Jewish Palestine the human body was banned, that is "untouchable," when it was unclean, leprous, or dead. Anyone who touched such a body transgressed ritual purity laws and became unclean; while unclean, a person could not participate in religious ceremonies.

In fulfilling the Mosaic law, Jesus also rejected many laws expanded by rabbinic interpretation. He allowed an unclean woman to touch him and was willing to touch a corpse and stop a funeral procession to help a woman. Nowhere is it recorded that after such occasions Jesus went through the regular Levitical procedures to make himself clean again. Of course, silence in the text does not necessarily prove this point.

One of the greatest miracles found in the four Gospels is the raising of the daughter of Jairus, the account of which is intertwined with the story of the woman with an issue of blood, an apparently incurable hemorrhage.[49] This is an episode within an episode, a literary device common to the Gospels. The two women's stories relate well to each other because the second woman was "dead" also. She could never have children, and her illness made her perpetually unclean; she was therefore a social outcast who could never take part in worship or social gathering.[50] In touching these two women, Jesus himself became unclean. In the case of Jairus' daughter, touching a dead body would result in uncleanness for seven days.[51]

In spite of social and religious prohibitions, Jesus touched both women and raised them to new life and the possibility of bearing children. The young girl, the daughter of Jairus, was twelve years old, and therefore legally able to marry. Both stories focus strongly on faith in Jesus despite impossible circumstances. The death-to-life theme is especially evident in both cases. The number twelve in both stories (twelve years of hemorrhage and twelve years old) emphasizes their similarity.

The great tragedy of the loss of his daughter is demonstrated by Jairus' anguished plea and the desperate mourning of family and friends. "And, behold, there cometh one of the rulers of the synagogue, Jairus by name; and when he saw him [Jesus], he fell at his feet, And besought him greatly, saying, My little daughter lieth at the point of death: I pray thee, come and lay thy hands on her, that she may live. And Jesus went with him; and much people followed, and thronged him."[52]

Implicit in Mark's account is that she was the only daughter and thus the last hope to carry on the family line—a matter in Jewish culture linked to life itself. Mourning for such a child would naturally be most acute and immediate. Of course, it was certain that many experienced such pain. As already noted, Jewish Palestine had a high infant mortality rate, typical of the time: nearly one-third of the live births were dead before age six. By the mid-teens, 60 percent would have died. This daughter was just becoming part of that 60 percent.

> There came from the ruler of the synagogue's house certain which said, Thy daughter is dead: why troublest thou the Master any further?
>
> As soon as Jesus heard the word that was spoken, he saith unto the ruler of the synagogue, Be not afraid, only believe.
>
> And he suffered no man to follow him, save Peter, and James, and John the brother of James.
>
> And he cometh to the house of the ruler of the synagogue, and seeth the tumult, and them that wept and wailed greatly.[53]

During the first century, women were hired as professional wailers, or mourners, to eulogize and bewail the dead. Calculated to stir the emotions of friends and family, mourning included loud weeping and wailing, playing flutes, beating the breast, wearing sackcloth, and lamenting the dead with a wavering, shrill cry. Matthew added, "And when Jesus came into the ruler's house, he saw the minstrels and the people making noise."[54] Even the poorest family was expected to have flute players and at least one wailing woman.

Upon his arrival, Jesus entered the courtyard (possibly) and forcibly ejected everyone except the mother and father and the three disciples who accompanied him: "And when he was come in, he saith unto them, Why make ye this ado, and weep? the damsel is not dead, but sleepeth. And they laughed him to scorn. But when he had put them all out, he taketh the father and the mother of the damsel, and them that were with him."[55]

He then bent slightly to pass through the low narrow doorway into the home directly "and entereth in where the damsel was lying. And he took the damsel by the hand, and said unto her, Talitha cumi; which is, being interpreted, Damsel, I say unto thee, arise. And straightway the damsel arose, and walked; for she was of the age of twelve years. And *they were astonished* with a great astonishment. And he charged them straitly that no man should know it; and commanded that something should be given her to eat."[56]

A superficial reading of Mark's account fails to see the people's deep reaction. The Greek here literally translated means, "they were all completely amazed." They understandably felt a profound sense of awe and surprise in the presence of one who had the right to raise the dead.

While on his way to Jairus's home, Jesus was followed by a large crowd. "And a certain woman, which had an issue of blood twelve years, And had suffered many things of many physicians and had spent all that she had, and was nothing bettered, but rather grew worse, When she had heard of Jesus, came in the press behind, and touched his garment."[57]

These few terse words, "had spent all that she had," reveal forcefully the economic impoverishment of the incurably ill in ancient society. She had been wealthy—since only those of sufficient resources sought out doctors during this period—but in the meantime had spent all her money on doctors who had been quite unable to heal her. By age thirty, most people's health was dreadful. Teeth were frequently rotted, eyesight was almost gone, and the effects of protein deficiency, internal parasites, and poor diet

were evident. Few poor people lived out their thirties. Impoverished, delivered over to her sick body and to social death, there
was no hope for this woman.

Luke, reportedly a physician, softened the description of the
woman's extensive medical treatment when he stated, "[She]
spent all her living upon physicians, neither could be healed of
any."[58] Any woman at the time would be willing to "spend all that
she had" to be cured of an illness that made her perpetually unclean; in consequence, everything she touched was also unclean.
Anyone sitting down where she had sat or touching a cloth she
had touched could become ritually unclean themselves. Having
exhausted all possible options, when "she had heard of Jesus,
[she] came in the press behind, and touched his garment. For she
said, If I may touch but his clothes, I shall be whole."[59] Jesus was
probably wearing a square upper garment or mantle on the cor-
ners of which would have been tassels as prescribed by Mosaic
law.[60] Matthew and Luke suggest that it was the tassels that the
woman touched.

In an environment where ritual impurity was seen as God's
punishment for sinful behavior, a woman with an "issue of blood
for twelve years" may have experienced a variety of abuses and es-
trangement from family and neighbors, such as those with leprosy
invariably did. Women—apparently in many cases on their own
initiative—refrained from entering the synagogue during menstruation, did not recite God's name, and did not look at the Torah
scrolls.

A woman during menstruation who passed between two men
was said to kill one of them if at the beginning of her period, and
if at the end, to cause strife between them. "The glance of a men-
struous woman poisons the air. . . . She is like a viper who kills
with her glance. How much more harm will she bring to a man
who sleeps with her."[61]

Everything she touched or anyone she touched would fall
under the same ritual defilement. This may explain why the woman,
according to Luke, "came behind him."[62] Touching Jesus was
doubly courageous, since it was both a breach of social codes for
proper female behavior and an infraction of Jewish religious law.

This story also underscores Jesus' attitude towards the importance of women. He was proceeding to the home of the male
leader of the synagogue, a position of respect and honor within

the community, but nevertheless attended to the needs of a woman who probably was excluded from that community in many ways.

The healing aspect of the story is not the primary concern of the story for this book but rather how Jesus responded to an unclean woman who violated religious custom by touching him without permission.

Immediately after the woman touched him, Jesus, "knowing in himself that virtue had gone out of him, turned him about in the press, and said, Who touched my clothes?"[63] Though moved by crowds, he was highly sensitive to the individual. The disciples' question, "Thou seest the multitude thronging thee, and sayest thou, Who touched me?" perhaps implies that often those who came to Jesus wished to touch him.[64] The disciples' query is not found in Matthew and is more deferential in Luke.[65] Jesus turned around "to see her that had done this thing."[66] Evidently the woman had attempted to hide herself in the crowd, but now as Jesus looked at her she became fearful and began to tremble, perhaps as a result of knowing that she had rendered Jesus ritually unclean. Admitting to the physical contact, she risks at least Jesus' rejection, if not his anger, but instead of condemning her for her act, he blessed her.

Jesus' open exchange with the woman (without letting the healing pass by unnoticed) can be understood as another attempt to teach his disciples a lesson about what "being on the outside looking in" really means and how the coming of the kingdom of God through him is a rejection of the Jews' religious intolerance.

As their eyes met, the woman came forward and "fell down before him, and told him all the truth."[67] Jesus' gentle and reassuring reply was, "Daughter, thy faith hath made thee whole; *go in peace*, and be whole of thy plague."[68] Calling her "daughter" may be a sign that she had been reintroduced into Abraham's family, since the Jews saw themselves as his children. Additionally, the use of the phrase, "go in peace" corresponds to the Hebrew of 1 Samuel 1; "Then Eli answered and said, *Go in peace*: And the God of Israel grant thee thy petition that thou hast asked of him."[69] The word *peace* is found only here in Mark. The Hebrew word *shalom* implies the meaning of soundness or wholeness, rather than the sense of an absence of strife and malice implied by the English translation.[70]

Jesus' teaching relating to women and their roles was sometimes reformative, but usually just controversial in its original setting. Even when the Gospel writers wrote their own stories, it is likely that the very reason they felt a need to stress Jesus' interaction with women in such a positive light was that their own audience had strong reservations about some of Jesus' views on the subject.

The case for women being seen as equal objects of God's love and equal examples for disciples, as well as being disciples, had still to be argued among some when these Gospels were written. Jesus' teaching must have had a special impact on the women in Israel and the women of the first century who heard his teaching through the written pages of the Gospels. It certainly had an impact on those who sat at his feet.

Jewish women usually sat silently in their segregated places in the synagogue, while men and male children could be called upon to read from the holy scriptures. They could not become disciples of a great rabbi or teacher. Jesus not only allowed them to sit at his feet but also encouraged them to do so.

Chapter Ten

They Sat at Jesus' Feet:
Women as Disciples

$\mathcal{M}$ary of Bethany had both a sister and a brother—Martha and Lazarus.[1] Mary often suffered the fate of many women—she lived in the shadow of others, in this case of Martha and Lazarus.[2] According to Luke, Mary sat at the Lord's feet and listened to his teaching.[3] Her demeanor, that is, her posture—indicated by a technical expression "to sit at the feet of," meaning "to be a disciple of"—and her listening clearly indicate that she was becoming Jesus' disciple.[4] He clearly extolled Mary's discipleship.[5]

"And now it came to pass, as they went, that he entered into a certain village: and a certain woman named Martha received him into her house. And she had a sister called Mary, which also sat at Jesus' feet, and heard his word."[6]

Although some rabbis agreed that daughters should be taught the scriptures (at least the Mosaic laws dealing with women, such as the trial of bitter water), many others believed that women were to be totally excluded from this most central of all aspects of Jewish religious life. According to one Jewish sage, "Let the words of the Torah rather be destroyed by fire than imparted to women."[7] Even if a woman studied them, they would not benefit her.[8] In fact, women were not permitted to even touch the scriptures in Jesus' day.

Even at the synagogue women came to hear but not to study or learn the scriptures. Instead of studying God's word, Jewish women earn merit before God "by making their children go to the synagogue to learn Scripture and their husbands to the Beth Hamidrash [weekday synagogue school for adult males] to learn

Midrash, and waiting for their husbands till they return from the Hamidrash."[9]

Furthermore, there is no indication that previous to Jesus' ministry, Jewish women were ever permitted to be disciples of a rabbi, much less travel with such a teacher or to instruct anyone other than children. From this story, it is obvious that Jesus rejected the traditions that barred women from Torah study. Jesus has returned to the original injunction in the law of Moses: "Gather the people together, men, and *women*, and children, and the stranger that is within thy gates, that they may hear, and that they may learn, and fear the Lord your God, and observe to do all the words of this law."[10]

Mary behaved like a male disciple of a male teacher or rabbi. As Jose ben Joezer of Zeredah, who lived ca. 160 B.C., said: "Let thy house be a meeting-house for the Sages and sit amid the dust of their feet and drink in their words with thirst."[11] Mary, as did the Samaritan woman at the well, sought to "drink in [Jesus'] words with thirst."

The significance of this story is enhanced when we recognize that it also fits into a repeated discipleship theme of hearing the word and doing it. Both the indication that Mary had "sat at Jesus' feet" and the statement that she "heard his word" showed her assuming the role of a disciple. She was clearly responding to Jesus' call to both hear his words and do them.[12] Mary's anointing of Jesus shortly before his death bears witness that his teachings to Mary had born fruit and she was now included in Jesus' family: "my mother and my brethren are these which hear the word of God and do it."[13]

Discipleship

Masculine plurals in the New Testament often encompass both men and women; therefore, terms such as *the disciples* likely include Jesus' male and female followers. However, some of Jesus' most difficult statements appear to relate to men only.

"And there went great multitudes with him: and he turned, and said unto them, If any man come to me, and hate not his father, and mother, and wife, and children, and brethren, and sisters, yea, and his own life also, he cannot be my disciple. And whosoever doth not bear his cross, and come after me, cannot be my disciple."[14]

Leaving one's sister in that culture would not necessarily have been seen as a sacrifice, for a sister was at best seen as a responsibility and more often as a burden. However, Jesus valued women enough to assume that leaving a sister would be as much a sacrifice as was leaving parents or children or houses.

Of course, Matthew terms the commandment in another way:

> Think not that I am come to send peace on earth: I came not to send peace, but a sword.
>
> For I am come to set a man at variance against his father, and the daughter against her mother, and the daughter in law against her mother in law.
>
> And a man's foes shall be they of his own household.
>
> He that loveth father or mother more than me is not worthy of me: and he that loveth son or daughter more than me is not worthy of me.
>
> And he that taketh not his cross, and followeth after me, is not worthy of me.
>
> He that findeth his life shall lose it: and he that loseth his life for my sake shall find it.[15]

The calling to discipleship appears only applicable to men for Luke states, "If any *man* come to me, and hate not his father, and mother, and *wife*, and children, and brethren, and sisters."[16] The Joseph Smith Translation (JST) expands the statement to include women: "If any man come to me, and hate not his father, and mother, and wife, and children, and brethren, and sisters, *or husband*, yea, and his own life also, *or in other words, is afraid to lay down his life for my sake*, cannot be my disciple."[17]

In the Gospels we find that Jesus gives an original meaning to the term *disciples* (*mathetes*).[18] With few exceptions, the term *disciple* is used in the New Testament solely for those who have recognized Jesus as their Master or Lord. Unlike Jewish students who asked a rabbi for permission to follow (and study with) him, Jesus did not ask his disciples if they could read, since he did not intend to introduce them to a rabbinic course in exegesis (the critical explanation or analysis of the scriptures).[19] Jesus had no apparent concern for such activity or ability on the part of the potential disciple. Ministry in the New Testament seems to be a specific

form of discipleship[20] in which the disciple performed the ministry
of the angels[21] and of Jesus himself.[22]

Jesus does have special requirements for his own disciples,
however. First, there is a call from Jesus himself. Jesus initiates
such calls. Second, there is a personal relationship and attachment
to Jesus himself. The verb "to follow" (*akolouthein*) is used to
designate this intimacy with Jesus.[23] Closely following Jesus re-
quires a complete break with one's past—a conversion.

When Jesus proclaimed the good news from God, he said:
"The time is fulfilled, and the kingdom of God is at hand: repent
ye, and believe the gospel."[24] The Greek verb for repent (*meta-
noeo*) means to "think over," to "gain insight" into one's life, and
to change what needs to be changed.[25]

For a sinner, changing one's mind or rethinking involves re-
penting or changing one's life; for a righteous person not conscious
of personal sin, the demand of repentance might better be translated as a change of mind, attitude, or motivation. To follow Jesus
is to conform to his behavior, to listen to his teachings, and to imi-
tate his life: "And when he had called the people unto him with
his disciples also, he said unto them, Whosoever will come after
me, let him deny himself, and take up his cross, and follow me.
For whosoever will save his life shall lose it; but whosoever shall
lose his life for my sake and the gospel's, the same shall save it."[26]

Third, the disciples of Jesus have the same destiny as their
Master, that is, they must carry their crosses daily and receive from
God the gift of the kingdom.[27]

Mark's Gospel presented Jesus to his audience (the recent
Gentile convert in the first century) as the ideal disciple, noting
especially his willingness to lay down his life. Early disciples of
Jesus had to contemplate possible persecution and martyrdom for
the sake of the gospel.

Mark assured these new converts that their suffering and possible death had meaning and were part of God's plan. Their suffering was also vital, for they had been told not to accept the pre-
dictions of some teachers that Christ was about to return in glory
and power to vindicate them by a triumphant victory over their
Roman adversaries and persecutors.

Jesus' first words to his disciples summarized and outlined
Mark's whole message. Jesus called Andrew, Peter, James, and
John as his first disciples and told them, "Come ye after me, and I

will make you to become fishers of men."[28] They, along with anyone else who chose to come, had to follow in Jesus' footsteps. He was the ideal Disciple and Master, but there are also other examples of discipleship within Mark's narrative; among them are women, some well-known and some obscure.

These stories, along with many others from the four Gospels, demonstrate that Jesus invited everyone to become disciples—women as well as men, prostitutes as well as Pharisees. The parable of the great supper jolts the hearer into recognizing this basic truth: everyone is invited to come into the kingdom to sit at Jesus' feet.[29]

Peter's Mother-in-Law (Mark 1:29–34; Matthew 8:14–17; Luke 4:38–41)

The first woman to appear in the Gospel of Mark is also the second person healed by Jesus as he began his ministry in Capernaum (the Latinization of the Hebrew *Kfar Nahum,* which means the village of Nahum).[30]

Identified by her connection to her closest living male relative, Simon Peter, she lived in the house with Peter and his brother Andrew. This residence probably became the new home of Jesus at Capernaum (a fishing village located on the northwest shore of the Sea of Galilee). The town's population was probably no more than 1,500 people at the time.

Jesus began this story by entering the local synagogue to teach.[31] On the Sabbath day, the service in the synagogue featured prayers, scripture reading, and teaching. Any male of sufficient learning could be invited to teach. The people present on the occasion were "astonished at his doctrine: for he taught them as one that had authority, and not as the scribes."[32] Jesus then healed a man with "an unclean spirit," and "immediately his fame spread abroad throughout all the region round about Galilee."[33]

Mark's narrative continues: "And forthwith, when they were come out of the synagogue, they entered into the house of Simon and Andrew, with James and John. But Simon's wife's mother lay sick of a fever, and anon [immediately] they tell him of her. And he came and took her by the hand, and lifted her up; and immediately the fever left her, and she *ministered* unto them."[34]

Archaeologists may have recently discovered the home Jesus entered on this day, located about thirty feet south of the synagogue where he may have taught.[35] The home represents an extended family residence or "clan" dwelling. These larger homes were arranged around internal courts, which numbered at times as many as three; around these courts were rooms which faced inward. Jesus entered the home through the single entrance to the house (inner courtyard), which faced the street and had a threshold and jambs with pins for the wooden door. From the courtyard Jesus entered into one of the rooms where Peter's mother-in-law laid sick.

Luke's version of the story varies slightly from the other synoptics, but his choice of words is significant. For Luke, sickness and demonic possession are viewed as oppressive constraints and bondage from which one must be released. In contrast to Matthew and Mark, Luke indicated that Simon's mother-in-law was "seized," "oppressed," or "ruled" by a great fever, implying confinement or constraint.[36] Jesus in this case "rebuked the fever." The same verb was used for Jesus' commanding of the unclean spirit earlier.[37] Jesus commanded the fever to "release her," part of the fulfillment of his Messianic call just revealed in Nazareth.[38] Hence, his mission is to both men and women, demonstrated by Jesus releasing both a man and a woman as he begins his mission.

The King James Version (KJV) of the Bible is remarkably clear on what Simon's mother-in-law does following Jesus' healing. Several other English-language versions translate the verb designating her action as "serve" or "wait," which is acceptable as long as the same translation has been used for this word in its first appearance in the story in Mark,[39] but some of those translations render the first occurrence as "the angels ministered to him." Translating the same Greek word as "minister" when angels are the subject, but "serve" or "wait" when a woman is the subject downplays her action.[40]

Mark, by using the same word for the action of angels and the action of the healed woman, may be attempting to equate her level of service to Jesus as that of the angels. What the angels were able to do for Jesus in the wilderness, the woman whose fever has now fled does for him in her home.

In this way, Peter's mother-in-law fulfills Jesus' instruction,

"Whosoever will be great among you, let him be your *minister;* And whosoever will be chief among you, let him be your *servant:* Even as the Son of man came not to be ministered unto, but to *minister*, and to give his life a ransom for many."[41]

Several aspects of the story deserve additional attention. First, according to first-century rabbinic interpretation of the fourth commandant, "Remember the sabbath day, to keep it holy," a physician was not to perform his duties unless it was a life-and-death situation. Otherwise, the physician was required to wait until the next day. Obviously, Jesus rejected this interpretation and performed the miracle without waiting until sunset, while others in the village who wanted to be healed waited until the evening after the Sabbath was over: "And at even, when the sun did set, they brought unto him all that were diseased, and them that were possessed with devils. And all the city was gathered together at the door [the courtyard doorway]. And he healed many that were sick of divers diseases, and cast out many devils; and suffered not the devils to speak, because they knew him."[42]

That Jesus willfully broke tradition here should not surprise anyone. For him, to do good, to heal, and to save life fulfilled the command to keep the Sabbath holy.

Simon Peter's mother-in-law, once healed, felt under no obligation to follow rabbinic regulation about hosting visitors on the Sabbath either. She ministered unto Jesus and those who were with him (the Greek text of Matthew states "ministered unto him.")

To suppose that Jesus healed this woman to find favor with Peter's wife so that he could leave his family to follow Jesus misses the point. He was interested in every individual during his mortal ministry and was unwilling to wait even a few hours unnecessarily to liberate an individual from suffering.[43]

The Samaritan Woman (John 4:4–42)

Although longer and inconvenient to do so, most Jews traveling from Jerusalem to Galilee would bypass the areas around Sychar in order to avoid the Samaritan population center. Jesus traveled through Samaria sometime in late December or early January on his way to Galilee.[44] On the second day of his journey from

Jerusalem, he arrived at Jacob's well (nearly forty miles from the holy city). In fact, prior to this story, his activity had centered on Jews and places of official Judaism.[45] When Jesus arrived in Samaria, Jews and Samaritans were bitter enemies.[46] The source of such enmity was a dispute about the correct place of worship, a problem the Samaritan woman herself puts before Jesus.[47] Although the break between Jews and Samaritans was first narrated in 2 Kings 17, the most intense rivalry began about 300 B.C.

The Samaritans built and worshiped at a religious shrine on Mount Gerizim, a shrine that competed with the temple in Jerusalem. For the Samaritans, Mount Gerizim was as sacred as Mount Moriah was for the Jews, and still remains so to this day. This shrine was eventually destroyed by Jewish troops in 128 B.C., an act that only further deepened animosity between them. The ample historical reasons for Judeans and Samaritans to dislike each other, were paralleled by the doctrinal disputes.

When Jesus met the Samaritan woman at the well, he met someone who provided a striking contrast to all those he met before. When Jesus spoke earlier with Nicodemus,[48] he spoke with a male member of the Jewish religious establishment, an educated man steeped in the traditions of the Jews. At the well, he spoke with a female member of an enemy people. Nicodemus had a name, but this woman is unnamed; she is known only as a foreign woman.

The conversation between Jesus and the woman was thus an extraordinary event, as the woman herself noted. She responded to Jesus' request for water with the words, "How is it that thou, being a Jew, askest drink of me, which am a woman of Samaria?"[49] The woman knew that a Jew would not consider drinking water from a Samaritan vessel; much less would a Jewish man talk with a Samaritan.[50]

Jesus' disciples noted the situation with some alarm and were clearly shocked, particularly because he was conversing in public with a woman. It is not simply that she is a Samaritan, or a woman, but a Samaritan woman. A first-century Jewish restriction warned that one could never count on the ritual purity of Samaritan women since they were menstruants from the cradle![51] While it was certainly a demeaning curse during the period for a Jew to be called a Samaritan, a Samaritan woman held even a lower status than a Samaritan male.[52]

John's often-used imagery of dark and light also appeared in these two contrasting stories.[53] First, Nicodemus "came by night," while the woman came to the well at "about the sixth hour," which is in the middle of the day. It was highly unusual for a Jewish leader to seek out Jesus at night, and it was rare for a woman to come to the well at noon in the heat of the day to accomplish a task usually done in the early morning and evening. In fact, women generally tried to avoid being outside during the busy times of day such as noon.

Nicodemus used the plural "we" when relating his feelings about Jesus, the woman on the other hand, used the singular "I." Nicodemus faded back into the night without the slightest hint of his reaction to Jesus' words, while the woman on the other hand departed from Jesus rejoicing and proclaiming his words to others.[54]

The central message in regards to this study that the story of the Samaritan woman is that she heard the word and responded. She returned to her village and told her neighbors, "Come, see a man," indicating that she not only told them about Jesus but also asked them to come back with her to hear and meet him. "Then they [including the woman] went out of the city, and came unto him."[55] This may explain why she left her heavy water pot at the well when she left Jesus—she knew that she would shortly return.

The account also suggests that a woman played a significant role in gaining the first Samaritan converts.[56] At first her neighbors in the city believed on her words: "And many of the Samaritans of that city believed on him for the saying of the woman," but later they "said unto the woman, Now we believe, not because of thy saying: for we have heard him ourselves, and know that this is indeed the Christ [the Messiah], the *Saviour of the world*."[57]

The move from believing that Jesus was a prophet to having faith that he was the long-expected Messiah (a prophet like Moses) eventually took on even greater significance—he was a more universal figure than their religion allowed for: "the Saviour of the world."[58]

Jesus willingly revealed his identity as Messiah to the woman and sent her back to her people, where her words bore fruit like the words of the disciples in other parts of the Gospels. Just as this woman was an instrument in extending the gospel to Samaritans, another encounter between Jesus and a non-Jewish woman began an extension beyond the narrow focus of the Jewish ministry.

The Syrophenician Woman (Mark 7:24–30; Matthew 15:21–28)

The Gospel of Mark presents an encounter between Jesus and a woman described as a "Greek, a Syrophenician," in which the woman begged Jesus to cast out a demon that had possessed her small daughter.[59] She probably was a Greek woman, born in Syrian Phoenicia. Matthew called her a Canaanite, which might indicate her religious affiliation. This woman had a notable place in introducing the second multiplication of loaves with its symbolism of a bread destined for the non-Jewish world.

The story hints at a special "insight" of the woman, since Jesus was hidden in a house and did not wish anyone to know about his presence.[60] Yet somehow the woman knew—she found out where he was and came to him for her daughter's healing despite the racial and religious barriers between non-Jews and Jews.

Jesus' response seems harsh, "Let the children [of Israel] first be filled: for it is not meet to take the children's bread, and to cast it unto the dogs [Gentiles]."[61] In Jewish Palestine, dogs were like pigs—scavengers who roamed the town dumps and streets for food. The dog was always spoken of in contempt, not as "man's best friend." It is reasonable to assume that Jesus' intent was to test the woman's faith.

Mark highlights the faith and humility of this woman, who trusted despite Jesus' apparent refusal. She replied, "Yes, Lord: yet the dogs under the table eat the children's crumbs."[62] She has the distinction of being singled out for direct praise from Jesus: "For this saying go thy way; the devil is gone out of thy daughter."[63] Her daughter's miracle is the only one worked from a distance in Mark's Gospel. The woman returned home and found her daughter lying in her bed, released from her prison of demonic possession. The deep faith of a Greek mother thus presented as a model of discipleship.

The story also demonstrates that Jesus accepted all who sincerely sought him. The one who here sought Jesus was not only a Gentile but also a woman. She was also without the respectability of a husband, and the mother of a daughter rather than a son, a condition sometimes so lamented in the ancient world that people who only had daughters were considered childless.

While the story is absent from the Gospel of Luke, it is preserved in the Gospel of Matthew, which identifies the woman as a Canaanite and has Jesus accede to the woman's request, praising her not for the character of her response but for the magnitude of her faith.[64] "Then Jesus answered and said unto her, O woman, great is thy faith: be it unto thee even as thou wilt. And her daughter was made whole from that very hour."[65] While the story in Mark ends without any further discussion, Matthew preserves the fact that she acknowledged Jesus as the Son of David.[66]

Martha of Bethany (Luke 10:38–42)

Inside a common home of Jesus' time, whether built of clay, stone, or basalt, was found a familiar scene. If it was a two-story home, the lower area was usually reserved for storage and for the care and feeding of smaller domestic animals. Even in a one-room stone house, a higher level was used for the family living area built over a stone arch, which provided a small animal shelter and stable area beneath. Either style dwelling was usually furnished with simple handcrafted articles. The one room in a simple home was cramped, dark, and smoky, since it served as kitchen, living area, and bedroom.

As soon as the evening meal was completed, the family cleared a space for the mats or mattresses used for sleeping. The roof was often a retreat for the family from the hot, crowded, and dimly lit room within their home. A parapet wall around the roof provided a safe haven for children's activities, while a rough shade booth in one corner of the roof offered relief from the hot summer sun.

A woman's life and duties centered around her home and family. Spinning was an important responsibility often completed in spare minutes. Sewing and mending of all kinds were constantly required since most people had few changes of clothing. Most clothes were made by the woman at home and were of simple cut.

Embroidery decorated the plain tunic of a woman, and occasionally that of a little girl. The nurturing of children (boys until they were five years of age, and girls until they were married at

twelve years of age) was the mother's responsibility. Gathering twigs and branches to be used for cooking and heating was a young girl's task. Daily sweeping the dirt floor (often mud and chipped rock hand-packed) was also a woman's job. Filling the lamps with oil was an essential daily duty. Washing clothes always took place at a nearby stream or pool. Obtaining fresh goat's milk, along with its by-products of butter and cheese, were the duties of women in the household. Daily shopping for fresh fruits and vegetables was usually done at a neighborhood market.

A woman's responsibility also included collecting fresh water from the local well or spring (at least twice daily, once in the early morning and again in the evening). Food preparation was the main concern of every wife and mother. Breakfast consisted of a handful of nuts, raisins, and some bread or olives. Usually cheese, bread, olives, and possibly a handful or two of parched grain served a family for lunch. The main meal, or evening meal, was often cooked stew, sometimes with meat, and a side dish of vegetables, fruit, and fresh bread. Occasionally fish, roasted meats, game, or dried and caked fruits, along with seasonally fresh fruits and vegetables, accompanied these simple dishes. Wine, honey, and dairy products were available year round.

Women spent much time preparing and sharing their "daily bread." In grain-rich Jewish Palestine, bread was indispensable. One kind of bread was a small, round loaf, and another was a thin, flat bread called "cakes." Before using grain from the storage bin and grinding it to a fine flour on a hand mill, they separated the grain from impurities with a sieve. To make dough, a flour and water mixture was worked in a kneading trough with yeast and set aside to rise.

The loaves were then put into a heated clay oven directly on the embers and watched with great care. The cakes, being very thin, could be baked on the outside of the oven, or on a small dish placed over hot coals. Because of the difficulty of preserving food in the warm climate, most food was purchased and prepared daily. Even bread was made every day, since it would become rough and dry after just one day.

We now return to the story of Martha and Mary found in Luke 10, this time looking at the story as Martha's, not Mary's. "Now it came to pass, as they went, that [Jesus] entered into a certain village: and a certain woman named Martha received him into her house."[67] The village was Bethany, located less than two miles from Jerusalem on the eastern slope of the Mount of Olives. Martha was apparently the elder of the two sisters in the household, since it was she who received Jesus into her house. It is not surprising, now that we have reviewed a woman's daily life, that "Martha was cumbered about much serving" when Jesus entered her home.[68]

Martha sacrifices for Jesus in two ways. First, she hosts him in her home, and second, she serves him a meal herself (both socially inappropriate actions, since a man was not to enter a home or be served by a woman who was not his wife or relative). Women did not normally eat with men whenever there was a guest present, nor did the women normally serve the men if a boy or a slave were available (apparently there was no help).

Martha obviously notices that her sister is not helping with their guest and asks, "Lord, dost thou not care that my sister hath left me to serve alone? bid her therefore that she help me."[69] Initially, Martha's request appears justifiable because it seems unfair for Mary not to help. Martha apparently suspected, as does the modern reader, that Jesus would grant her petition. Jesus' unexpected reply, though gentle, makes a powerful statement. Jesus responds, "Martha, Martha, thou art careful and troubled about many things: But one thing is needful: and Mary hath chosen that good part, which shall not be taken away from her."[70]

There may not be a more difficult story in Luke's entire Gospel for female disciples today to understand than this one. Many women have long been uncomfortable with this familiar story. There certainly is no agreement about its basic meaning in any commentary or discussions. People respond to it differently, often passionately. Women in the Church today are often identified as being "a Martha" or "a Mary." Many women relate deeply with Martha, and others equally as deeply with Mary. Some resolve the conflict by suggesting that at one time a woman needs to be a Martha and at other times a Mary.

Others see the issue as being a question of priorities. How many times does someone have Jesus at her home? Martha should have been prepared for Jesus' visit, so that she too could have sat at his feet.

The Greek text emphasizes that Martha was "anxious" and "distracted about many things," probably including Mary's choice to sit at Jesus' feet while Martha continued to work.[71] She wanted to rectify the situation by having Mary come and help her; however, Jesus surprised Martha by telling her that there was one necessity (hearing the word). Mary had chosen it, and Jesus would not take it away from her. Perhaps Jesus wanted Martha to understand that although many things distracted her, there was only one necessary focus—that of being a disciple.

It is obvious that Jesus showed concern for physical nourishment as exemplified in the feeding of the five and four thousand. When he raised Jarius' daughter from the dead he told her parents "that something should be given her to eat."[72] Yet Jesus on another occasion warned about anxiety regarding physical needs.[73] In this light, true discipleship consists not of caring for temporal needs but rather of a willingness to be hearers of the word. Mary's discipleship is not to be overshadowed by Martha's altruistic service.

Another possible interpretation also exists. Instead of being rebuked by Jesus, Martha was being called to discipleship. The repeated "Martha, Martha" is reminiscent of earlier calls from the Lord. When God spoke to Jacob (Israel) in Beersheba he said, "Jacob, Jacob. And he said, Here am I."[74] Later, when the Lord called Samuel he said, "'Samuel! Samuel!' He answered, 'Here I am'."[75] And finally, Jesus himself called Saul (Paul) on the road to Damascus to discipleship, "And he fell to the earth, and heard a voice saying unto him, Saul, Saul."[76]

When Jesus called his first disciples he asked them to leave their work and follow him:

> Now as he walked by the sea of Galilee, he saw Simon and Andrew his brother casting a net into the sea: for they were fishers.
> And Jesus said unto them, Come ye after me, and I will make you to become fishers of men.
> And straightway they forsook their nets, and followed him.
> And when he had gone a little further thence, he saw James the son of Zebedee, and John his brother, who also were in the ship mending their nets.
> And straightway he called them: and they left their father Zebedee in the ship with the hired servants, and went after him.[77]

That others were called to leave all and follow is demonstrated numerous times in the Gospels.[78]

We know that certain women left their homes in Galilee and followed Jesus during his journey throughout Jewish Palestine, including Mary Magdalene, Joanna, Susanna, and many others.[79] Are Jesus' words, "Martha, Martha" such a call—an invitation to leave her family and friends and the duties required of her as the householder and follow Jesus full time as others have already done?

In any case, Jesus did not come to be served, but to serve. He in actuality was the host, and Mary and Martha were his guests.

Mary, Martha, and Jesus (John 11:1–46)

The account of the raising of Lazarus is only a small part of a larger story. Of the forty-four verses that constitute this story, only seven take place at Lazarus's tomb.[80] The miracle of raising Lazarus from the dead is the climax of this story, but it is not its center, for as John stated, "Now Jesus loved Martha, and her sister, and Lazarus."[81]

The focus of John's story centers around the conversation that Jesus had with Martha and Mary on the way to the tomb. The story begins when Martha and Mary sent Jesus a message about their brother's illness.[82] When Jesus finally arrived at the family home, Lazarus had been entombed four days.[83]

Customs practiced by close relatives of the deceased included intense mourning, which started with the burial and lasted seven days (known as *Shivah*) as the family members continued to express their grief, often at the tomb itself. The wail of mourners was especially strident on the day of burial and for the following two days. The family also abstained from washing and anointing and from wearing footwear and ornaments. Garments were rent (torn), sackcloth worn, heads covered, and the mourners sat on the bare ground or low couches. Lamentations were chanted, and all pleasurable activity ceased. For these seven days, mourners received the condolences of relatives and friends.[84] "And many of the Jews came to Martha and Mary, to comfort them concerning their brother."[85]

When word of Jesus' imminent approach reached Martha and Mary, Martha went first to greet him, while Mary stayed at home.[86] While it is certain that Martha's words to Jesus expressed complaint, they also exuded confidence, "Lord, if thou hadst been here, my brother had not died. But I know, that even now, whatsoever thou wilt ask of God, God will give it thee."[87] Martha is portrayed as a faithful disciple. As such, it was her right to "ask what ye will, and it shall be done unto you."[88] Jesus told the grieving sister that her brother would rise again. At first Martha understood Jesus' words as having reference to the belief in the resurrection of the body held by some Jews at the time.

At this point some of Jesus' most powerful words recorded in the New Testament fall from his lips, "I am the resurrection, and the life: he that believeth in me, though he were dead, yet shall he live: And whosoever liveth and believeth in me shall never die."[89] When asked if she believed his announcement, she responded in faith, "Yea, Lord: I believe that thou art the Christ, the Son of God, which should come into the world."[90] This is the closest parallel to Peter's confession in scripture. Most significant, it was offered by a woman disciple.[91]

Upon Martha's return home, she quietly summoned Mary to Jesus. Mary spoke to Jesus with the same forthrightness that her sister had demonstrated earlier. Mary also mourned before Jesus. Her weeping touched Jesus, and when he finally reached Lazarus' tomb, he also wept.[92] At the tomb, Jesus ordered the stone to be removed against Martha's will. Upon Jesus' command, Lazarus came forth.[93]

The Women of Jerusalem (Matthew 21:8; Mark 11:8; Luke 19:36; John 12:12–13; Luke 23:27–28)

The three synoptic Gospel writers agree that when Jesus arrived in Jerusalem for Passover during his last fateful week, a multitude met him on the slopes of the Mount of Olives and spread clothing and blankets before him.[94] John, however, adds to the story:

> On the next day much people that were come to the feast, when they heard that Jesus was coming to Jerusalem,
>
> Took branches of palm trees, and went forth to meet him, and cried, Hosanna: Blessed is the King of Israel that cometh in the name of the Lord.

And Jesus, when he had found a young ass, sat thereon; as it is written,

Fear not, daughter of Sion [Zion]: behold, thy King cometh, sitting on an ass's colt.[95]

The garments and branches spread on the road formed a carpet so that the feet of the colt did not even touch the soil or stones that ordinarily would have been trod. Palm branches had been a symbol of Jewish independence and freedom when the procession greeted the political and military victories of the Maccabees (beginning in ca. 175 B.C.). However, Jesus entered not as a military Messiah on a horse but on an ass as a symbol of peace and salvation. Ironically, the peaceful, nonpolitical nature of his kingdom that he openly proclaimed would later be violently rejected by many of those who hailed him on this day.

Most Jewish Palestinian inhabitants probably made at least one pilgrimage a year, the most popular festival being Passover. Those living in Jerusalem were already there, augmented by an additional 250,000 Palestinian Jews, plus a large number ("tens of thousands") of pilgrims from the Diaspora (non-Palestinian settlements of Jews). Herod's Temple, it has been estimated, could accommodate nearly 400,000 pilgrims for the festival daily. The reception may have been tremendous on this occasion with so many visitors in the city, many from Galilee where Jesus' mission had been so successful.

Entering as the Prince of Peace on this day, he left the walls of Jerusalem less than a week later as a condemned criminal. In an incident recorded by Luke alone, a sympathetic group of women followed him as he staggered under the load of the cross with the death wail of funeral mourners:

And there followed him a great company of people, and of women, which also bewailed and lamented him.

But Jesus turning unto them said, Daughters of Jerusalem, weep not for me, but weep for yourselves, and for your children.

For, behold, the days are coming, in the which they shall say, Blessed are the barren, and the wombs that never bare, and the paps which never gave suck.

Then shall they begin to say to the mountains, Fall on us; and to the hills, Cover us.

For if they do these things in a green tree, what shall be done in the dry?[96]

Jesus recognized the sincerity of these women, but he cautioned them in one last frightening beatitude to reserve their compassion for those who would need it most—themselves. For if a man whom Roman justice had pronounced innocent was condemned to die, what must the guilty expect in the onslaught of Roman military power? Even in the face of an agonizing and humiliating death, Jesus showed concern and compassion for the faithful women who followed him out of the city gates to Calvary.[97]

Mary the Mother of Jesus (John 2:1–11; 19:25–27)

John's Gospel has no birth narrative and introduces the mother of Jesus at a wedding in Cana, a small town possibly eight miles from Nazareth.[98] We find the Savior in an intimate, personal, familial setting—a wedding party.[99] He attended the wedding with his first disciples, along with his mother.[100] John indicates that Jesus "was called ['invited' in Greek]" to the wedding.[101] He is not the host of the wedding celebration, but a guest.[102]

The catalyst for Jesus' first public miracle—the changing of the water into wine—was his mother, Mary. When the wine at the wedding feast ran out, Mary informed Jesus of the situation. The conversation between Mary and her son was pivotal. When Jesus' mother spoke to him, "They have no wine," she asked nothing explicit of him, but Jesus' response, "Woman, what have I to do with thee? mine hour is not yet come," made clear that her words contained an implied request.[103]

Mary obviously assumed that Jesus could rectify the host's embarrassing situation. To the modern ear, Jesus' reply to his mother might seem harsh. The term *woman* is a form of address Jesus used on other occasions and certainly contains none of the disrespect that the English word has come to possess. His words were, in fact, not rude in the slightest way but rather declared to all faithful disciples that he was free from all human control, even that of his mother.[104]

That we should not interpret Jesus' words as rude is confirmed by Mary's response, "His mother saith unto the servants, Whatsoever he saith unto you, do it."[105] Mary told the servants with complete confidence that Jesus would do something. A model disciple, she trusted that Jesus would act and then allowed him to act in freedom.

The miracle that Jesus performed was appropriate to the personal setting of the wedding celebration. "There were set there six water pots of stone, . . . containing two or three firkins apiece [a firkin was nearly nine gallons]."[106] Jesus commanded the servants to fill the stone jars with water and then turned it into wine, somewhere between one hundred and one hundred and fifty gallons.[107] Turning water into wine was an act of turning scarcity into abundance and repaid the initial hospitality of being invited to the wedding feast. Jesus' first miracle as recorded in John took place in the presence of friends and family, not in the presence of Jewish and Roman leaders. This opening miracle showed that God's miraculous life-giving power was at work even (and perhaps, especially) in ordinary people's daily lives.[108]

Mary appeared again in only a few situations until her son was executed, where she again played a prominent role (especially in the Gospel of John). When she is mentioned in the Gospels, Mary appears with her other children.[109] In one reference we learn about her family from a disbelieving neighbor. Referring to Jesus, "Is this not the carpenter's son? is not his mother called Mary? and his brethren, James, and Joses [the Galilean pronunciation of Joseph], and Simon, and Judas? And his sisters, are they not all with us?"[110]

Mary and Joseph (both probably under twenty when Jesus was born) had children following the birth of her firstborn son. This is implied in Matthew: "Then Joseph being raised from sleep did as the angel of the Lord had bidden him, and took unto him his wife: And knew her not till she had brought forth her firstborn son."[111]

It appears that Jesus' brothers and sisters did not recognize his prophetic mission during his ministry. "His brethren therefore said unto him, Depart hence, and go into Judaea, that thy disciples may see the works that thou doest. . . . For neither did his brethren believe in him."[112] The significance of a verse in Mark is somewhat disputed.[113] The King James Version (KJV) renders the verse, "And when [Jesus'] friends heard of it, they went out to lay hold on him: for they said, He is beside himself." The Greek is very strong and definite: they set out "to take charge" (*kratesai*)—a verb used several times in two chapters of Mark with the meaning "to arrest."[114] The New International Version (NIV) translates the verse, "When his family heard about this, they went to take charge of him, for they said, 'He is *out of his mind.*'"[115]

While it is certainly unknown what Mary's reaction to this situation may have been or what the emotional struggle of family life might have been under these circumstances, Jesus understood his relationship with his brothers and sisters quite well: "But Jesus said unto them, A prophet is not without honour, but in his own country, and among his own kin, and in his own house."[116]

Mary next appeared at the foot of the cross, with a group of other women and one male disciple, presumably John. Jesus predicted that all the followers would abandon him at his death, scattering to their homes, but these women stood firm.[117] In the face of death and the fear of reprisals, they did not run away: "Now there stood by the cross of Jesus his mother, and his mother's sister, Mary the wife of Cleophas, and Mary Magdalene. When Jesus therefore saw his mother, and the disciple standing by, whom he loved, he saith unto his mother, Woman, behold thy son! Then saith he to the disciple, Behold thy mother! And from that hour that disciple took her unto his own home."[118]

Why Jesus asked the disciple to take Mary home may never be known; but, in all likelihood, now that her firstborn son's death approached, she had no one in her immediate family to rely on, as her other children had apparently rejected their older half-brother's mission and had possibly rejected her for following him. Joseph, who had not been mentioned since Jesus' trip to the temple when he was twelve years of age, presumably was dead.

Our last reference to Mary in the New Testament is found in the book of Acts: "And when [the Twelve] were come in, they went up into an upper room, where abode both Peter, and James, and John, and Andrew, Philip, and Thomas, Bartholomew, and Matthew, James the son of Alphaeus, and Simon Zelotes, and Judas the brother of James. These all continued with one accord in prayer and supplication, with the women, and Mary the mother of Jesus, and with his brethren."[119]

Mary, Jesus' mother, was the first believer, and her presence among the disciples following Jesus' ascension began a new chapter in the life of the Church. She became a bridge between the birth of her son and the birth of the Church he established—a living witness to the good news that he brought.

Chapter Eleven

Certain Women Which Had Been Healed: Female Disciples Who Followed Him

*J*esus and his disciples almost always traveled by foot and so did not need to make much use of roads suitable for wheeled traffic; there was no scarcity of pedestrian trails for them to follow as they went from place to place. Our usual image of twelve men, and maybe a few more, following Jesus does not take into account that "certain women" also followed him.

Certain Women (Luke 8:1–3)

"And it came to pass afterward, that he went throughout every city and village, preaching and shewing the glad tidings of the kingdom of God: and the twelve were with him, And certain women, which had been healed of evil spirits and infirmities, Mary called Magdalene, out of whom went seven devils, And Joanna the wife of Chuza Herod's steward, and Susanna, and many others, which ministered unto him of their substance."[1]

When male disciples were called to leave their homes, families, and occupations to follow Jesus, everything was understandable, obvious, and clear within the existing social customs. But then comes Luke's brief statement about the women who did the same—something totally unexpected. Women did indeed leave their homes in Jewish Palestine, but only to travel to feasts, visit family, or attend to business, and this was only for a short duration. Women leaving behind family responsibilities would have been considered extremely atypical.

It is certain that in this aspect of Jesus' mission, he broke not only with rabbinic Judaism (represented by the Pharisees) of his time but also with the Essenes. Too often comparisons have been made between the modern Church and the Dead Sea Scroll sect. Any similarities between the latter and early Christianity, much less the Church today, are dwarfed by the dissimilarities. Several allusions to the Essenes' beliefs and Jesus rejection of them have been preserved in the four Gospels.[2] In particular, association with commoners and even with lepers, the outcast, and women were actions that the Essenes would have considered an anathema. In contrast, Jesus visited, taught, and invited members of these groups to accept the kingdom of God he presented, in contrast to the "Teacher of Righteousness" the Essenes held up as the model of holiness and purity.

Women were not only included in Jesus' teachings but also incorporated in his group of disciples; he considered them his friends, taught them scripture, and broke Jewish prohibitions by conversing with Gentile women.

Mary Magdalene

Mary (Miriam) Magdalene, from the west bank of the Sea of Galilee, was a prominent disciple of Jesus. She is not to be confused with Mary of Bethany nor the "sinner" who anointed Jesus in the home of the Pharisee, as has been common since the Middle Ages.[3] She was known simply as Mary; her surname comes from her home town of Magdala.

We are not sure when Mary became a disciple of Jesus, but we do know that Jesus went to the area on several occasions. For example, Matthew notes that on one occasion Jesus entered a ship and went to the "coasts of Magdala."[4]

Magdala was a commercial town with a large fishing fleet that brought the inhabitants security and prosperity. It was located at the southern end of the Plain of Gennesaret on the western shore of the Sea of Galilee to the north of Tiberias. However, for those who lived under the black veil of mental disorder or psychological depression and attacks, such a community would offer little security or compassion.

Mary seems to have exhibited the symptoms of a serious mental or emotional illness. Although Luke and Mark only mention that Jesus healed her by casting seven devils out of her,[5] we can suppose that Jesus did with her as he had done with others before: he touched her, perhaps embraced her, and made her get up, like Peter's feverish mother-in-law or the person possessed by demons. He then spoke to her, and she had a tangible feeling of nearness and contact with him. As he spoke, the evil spirits left her. She again became herself, free to feel and decide, free once again to experience the world around her, free to enjoy herself and to learn to live again. But she did not return to her old ways. She left her prosperous home town of Magdala, even though she would always bear its name.

Mary's discipleship affected her whole existence. She surrendered herself completely to a new way of life by following Jesus. As Jesus had ministered to her, she now devoted herself to ministering to him. We do not know much about Mary, but she evidently had financial resources to help Jesus with his work.[6]

She must have had some leadership qualities and played a leading role among the women who followed Jesus, since all four Gospels always mention her first when they speak of this group of women. She had yet one more privileged position: the risen Jesus appeared to her and gave her the task of reporting his resurrection to the group of despairing disciples.

Joanna

When John the Baptist preached repentance to Herod Antipas (King Herod's son) because Herod had married Herodias, his brother's wife, a tremor was felt in the palace of the tetrarch of Galilee.[7] Among those that heard John's message of repentance and judgement was Joanna, the wife of Chuza, Herod's steward (*epitropos*). Chuza's title is used only here by Luke and probably means manager or minister of Herod's estates.[8]

At a time and place unknown to us, she heard Jesus and was healed by him. She left her luxurious surroundings, the intrigues of court life, and her slaves so that she could follow him. Joanna has been completely ignored by most of us. When she does appear

in our writings, Joanna is quickly passed over, while other person-
alities mentioned as briefly as she is (Joseph of Arimathea for example) have found a place in our literature.

Joanna was unique among Jesus' disciples—a person from
court society, a wife of a senior royal official, a woman who gave
up a position in the political center of Galilee for Jesus' cause. Was
she Chuza's widow and therefore in a position to use her resources to help finance Jesus' mission? Or was she a sick woman
no longer attractive enough for court ceremonies or to be a repre-
sentative of her husband? We do not know.

We do know something of that court and those whom Herod
employed, however. The palace at Tiberias, on the western shore
of the Sea of Galilee, was a beautiful residence built on the hill
that overlooked the city. Herod moved his residence there in A.D.
20 from Sepphoris, the largest city in Galilee. The new govern-
mental city was named in honor of the Roman emperor at the
time, Tiberius (A.D. 14–37). For a number of reasons, many Jews
found the city "unclean," and it became a Gentile city.

Mark has portrayed the dramatic scene in which Herodias's
daughter Salome (her name is given by Josephus, not the New
Testament) danced before her stepfather and the court with such
seduction that Herod, deeply affected, promised her up to half his
kingdom. Of course, we all know that at her urging of her
mother, she asked only for the head of John the Baptist. We have
no idea if Joanna was a witness of these events. The court was certainly aware of Jesus' movements and his connection to John the
Baptist.

When Jesus was finally arrested in Jerusalem, Pilate sent him
to Herod, who was in Jerusalem at the time. Herod had heard
stories of miracles and wanted to see one himself. Presumably one
of the miracles he had heard about was the healing of his minister's wife, Joanna.[9]

She had lived in an atmosphere of greed, caprice, wealth, political power, and indifference to those in need. Joanna's encounter with Jesus introduced her to something else, maybe for
the first time. When she left Herod's court, Joanna brought a degree of wealth of her own, and she apparently remained a respectable woman with influence and financial resources. The difference was that she was converted to Jesus' mission and life. Her
appearance among the group might explain how expensive oils

used for embalming and a meal and comfortable room for the Last Supper were found, since it seems unlikely that anyone else in the group could have afforded the price. In this, she might have provided some comfort to Jesus.

While she found a new life through Jesus' message, she probably never totally escaped her past. She always remained in danger as a former member of the royal court who now was associating with Jesus, considered by Herod as a traitor to the state. Nicodemus came by night, but Joanna stood with Jesus in broad daylight—at the cross and at the tomb on Easter morning with the other women.

Salome

Salome was among the female disciples who followed Jesus from Galilee to Jerusalem. A careful examination of the four Gospels helps us determine who she might have been and what role she might have played in Jesus' ministry.

Matthew tells us that at the cross were many individuals, "among which was Mary Magdalene, and Mary the mother of James and Joses, and the mother of Zebedee's children."[10] Mark reports that many women were present: "There were also women looking on afar off: among whom was Mary Magdalene, and Mary the mother of James the less and of Joses, and Salome."[11] Luke states that "all his acquaintance, and the women that followed him from Galilee, stood afar off, beholding these things."[12]

He reports that they saw where Jesus' body was laid and then returned upon the first day of the week bringing spices, even "Mary Magdalene, and Joanna, and Mary the mother of James, and other women that were with them."[13] John describes the same group in another way: "Now there stood by the cross of Jesus his mother, and his mother's sister, Mary the wife of Cleophas, and Mary Magdalene."[14]

All four Gospels report this important group of disciples at the cross. When placed in order, the list may help reveal their identity. It is probable that Salome in Mark is the same as the mother of Zebedee's children in Matthew and the sister of Jesus' mother in John. Given that sisters would not likely have the same name (Mary), John is probably identifying four different women instead of three as is commonly held. Therefore, it appears that Jesus' "mother's sister" and "Mary the wife of Cleophas" are two separate individuals.

Salome's husband, Zebedee, was a fisherman in Capernaum in Galilee and was closely associated in the business with Simon Peter and his brother Andrew.[15] He was of some means, since he had hired servants.[16] Salome may have contributed financially to Jesus' mission, for she "also, when he was in Galilee, followed him, and ministered unto him."[17]

During one of these journeys, she asked Jesus for a special favor. Luke indicates that "there was also a strife among [the Twelve], which of them should be accounted the greatest."[18] Matthew reveals the background of the strife: "Then came to him the mother of Zebedee's children with her sons, worshipping him, and desiring a certain thing of him. And he said unto her, What wilt thou? She saith unto him, Grant that these my two sons may sit, the one on thy right hand, and the other on the left, in thy kingdom."[19] Matthew continues, "And when the ten heard it, they were moved with indignation against the two brethren [James and John]."[20]

Two aspects of ancient society may explain this mother's behavior. First, Jewish women saw their whole worth embodied in their sons. She fell on her knees before Jesus (worshiping connotes this position) and asked him if she could make a special request. Her two grown sons stood beside her, interested in the outcome. Jesus encouraged the mother to make the request, and she asked what all mothers desire for their children, admiration and achievement. Jewish women enjoyed great respect as mothers of sons: "Sons are a heritage from the Lord, children a reward from him. Like arrows in the hands of a warrior are sons born in one's youth," we read in the book of Psalms.[21]

Second, Greco-Roman society organized itself in certain and distinct modes. The mother still clung to that to which this society attached value—power and prominence. While her request was placed in Old Testament language, Jesus' response made it clear that it was understood in Greco-Roman terms.

Jesus responded to her request: "The kings of the Gentiles exercise lordship over them; and they that exercise authority upon them are called benefactors. But ye shall not be so: but he that is greatest among you, let him be as the younger; and he that is chief, as he that doth serve. For whether is greater, he that sitteth at meat, or he that serveth? is not he that sitteth at meat? but I am among you as he that serveth."[22]

In the Greco-Roman world, society was organized based on patron-client relationships. Patronage was a social system marked by informal relations of inequality and reciprocity and was part of a hierarchical organization that established vertical ties between classes. Benefactors (*euergetes*) was the title used in the Hellenistic world for rulers and powerful individuals who gave money or gifts to the gods, their city, or their clients.[23] It was a rough equivalent of Roman *patronus*.[24] Their generosity—"euergetism"—was exercised to demonstrate and justify their own importance, not to help remove inequities.

Jesus rejected the word (*euergetes*) and what it stood for. Salome's natural question, given the social background of the culture, was used by Jesus to teach his disciples the principle of service within the kingdom and demonstrated the difference between his kingdom and the kingdoms of the world.

Salome's story does not end here with a hard lesson learned. Both Matthew and Mark recorded her presence at the cross with the familiar group of women. The mother of the sons of Zebedee (sons who fled—like all the other men at Gethsemane) remained faithful in the face of possible arrest.

We know little of the other women mentioned, particularly Susanna. She is mentioned here by name, but nowhere else. But she, along with many other women, followed Jesus to Jerusalem for the last time and watched him humiliated and finally crucified by Roman soldiers. "And all his acquaintance, and *the women that followed him* from Galilee, stood afar off, beholding these things."[25]

Chapter Twelve

A Memorial of Her:
A Woman Anoints Jesus

In Mark's passion narrative, three disciples play a major role in the story of Jesus' final week. The first two were members of the Twelve, Peter who denied Jesus and Judas who betrayed him. The third disciple, unnamed by Mark, anointed Christ in preparation for his burial.

Mark's Unnamed Woman (Mark 14:3–9)

While the accounts of Peter and Judas during Jesus' final days are engraved upon the institutional memory of Christianity and the Church, the story of the woman who anointed Jesus is virtually forgotten. She was an ideal disciple—one who understood who Jesus was and acted accordingly. Peter had declared Jesus to be both Messiah and Son of God but was rebuked for his failure to connect it with Isaiah's suffering servant—a servant who suffered and died.[1]

Peter, who represented all the Twelve, fundamentally misunderstood Jesus' mission. Peter, along with the others, could not bring himself to imagine that Jesus' mission might end with suffering and death.[2] He protested when Jesus spoke of his death; fear seized him and the rest as they came to Jerusalem:[3] "And they were in the way going up to Jerusalem; and Jesus went before them: and they were amazed; and as they followed, they were afraid. And he took again the twelve, and began to tell them what things should happen unto him."[4]

However, the woman of Bethany reacts differently. She not only anointed Jesus' head as a king but also understood his messianic kingship in terms of his coming suffering and death. It should be noted, however, that even this woman (and this seems to apply to all who followed Jesus from Galilee) did not understand that Jesus would resurrect three days following his death. So even she, along with all the disciples, had only a partial understanding of God's timetable and plan; nevertheless she stands above the rest.

Matthew's Unnamed Woman (Matthew 26:6–13)

Matthew begins his story of the anointing on an ominous note: "And it came to pass, when Jesus had finished *all* these sayings, he said unto his disciples, Ye know that after two days is the feast of the passover, and the Son of man is betrayed to be crucified. Then assembled together the chief priests, and the scribes, and the elders of the people, unto the palace of the high priest, who was called Caiaphas, And consulted that they might take Jesus by subtilty, and kill him."[5]

With its addition of the term *all* to the formula that concluded each of Jesus' previous teaching discourses—the Sermon on the Mount, the missionary discourse, the parable discourse, and the community discourse, the announcement that Jesus had "finished *all* these sayings" brought to a solemn conclusion not only the fifth and final major discourse but also "all" the words of Jesus' previous teachings.[6] The end was near.

In this setting, Jesus returned to Bethany and appeared at the home of Simon the leper.[7] The story that follows, with very minor variations, is that of Mark, one of Matthew's sources. The point of the story is obvious enough: Jesus knew already that he would be put to death by crucifixion and that he would be buried without the customary preparation for burial immediately following his death.

The customary preparation went as follows. The eyes were closed, the entire body was washed and anointed with oil, and the hands and feet were then wrapped in linen bands. The body, clothed in a favorite garment, was then wrapped around with winding sheets. Spices of myrrh and aloes were placed in the folds of the garment to perfume the body. A napkin was then bound from the chin to the head, and the body was laid out for viewing in an upper room.

For Jesus, there would be no time for the anointing between death and burial. Matthew informs us that several women went to the tomb to perform the ritual but found on arrival that Jesus was already risen.[8]

Mary of Bethany (John 12:1–8)

John not only provided a name—Mary—for the unknown woman of Matthew and Mark but also added significant information about the event. Between the raising of Lazarus and this story, John tells about the conspiracy to kill Jesus. His enemies have determined to capture him at the upcoming feast, knowing full well that Jesus will come up to Jerusalem to worship and teach. Thus, in the face of his own impending death, Jesus came to dine with those he loved at Bethany.[9] Bethany "was nigh unto Jerusalem, about fifteen furlongs off [about one and a third mile]."[10]

"Then Jesus six days before the passover came to Bethany, where Lazarus was which had been dead, whom he raised from the dead. There they made him a supper; and Martha served: but Lazarus was one of them that sat at the table with him."[11]

While the King James Version of the Bible (KJV) states that Jesus and Lazarus "sat at the table," the Greek text indicates that they followed Greco-Roman custom and "reclined" or laid on a mat while leaning on the left arm, thereby keeping the right hand free for eating the food placed on a low table.[12]

Martha served the meal, while Lazarus ate with Jesus, and Mary, who was mentioned last, was again at Jesus' feet (a position she took in each of the three stories where she appears in the Gospels).[13]

"Then took Mary a pound of ointment of spikenard, very costly, and anointed the feet of Jesus, and wiped his feet with her hair: and the house was filled with the odour of the ointment."[14]

Mary took the flask of very expensive perfume and poured it over Jesus' feet, who was reclining beside her brother on the cushions round the table. All of the elements of devotion and worship are present in her service—respect, affection, and tenderness. And even that was not enough; she wiped away the dust and oil from

First-century Judean terra-cotta bottles, used for such purposes as storing
perfumed oil or a day's supply of olive oil

Jesus' tired and dusty feet with her hair. That was the task of the
lowliest slave: the master at the table used to wipe his dirty hands
on the slave's hair.

Such service may be incompressible to many women today—
she does what no man would do—and it may have even shocked
Martha and Lazarus. All present might have been transfixed and
dumbfounded at these actions that represented Mary's own way
of showing love and devotion.

John emphasizes the fact that Mary's act was an extravagant
one: "a pound of ointment of spikenard, *very costly*." This is underscored by the comment that the entire "house was filled with
the odour" of the perfume. This ointment, made of pure nard is a
fragrant oil derived from the root and spike (hair stem) of the
nard plant, which grows in the mountains of northern India. The
depth of Mary's love for Jesus was signified by the extravagance of
her gift—the sweet smell of which filled the house. Through
Judas, we learn that Mary had spent nearly a year's wages on this
gesture (300 pieces of silver; Mark spoke of more than three hundred).[15] She anointed Jesus so profusely that all present could participate in it to some extent.

The disciples, with Judas as voice, protested the apparent extravagance and waste: "Why was not this ointment sold for three hundred pence, and given to the poor?"[16]

Mark's account emphasizes the anger of the disciples: "And there were some that had indignation within themselves, and said, Why was this waste of the ointment made? For it might have been sold for more than three hundred pence, and be given to the poor. And they *murmured* against her."[17] The word translated *murmured* relates to the snort of horses, so in English the sense is of persons "snorting with inward rage or indignation."[18]

Mary's generosity was set off against Judas's avarice, his pettiness against her large-heartedness. Judas (and the disciples) might have been attempting to create a sort of either-or situation: either you love Jesus or you love the poor. Jesus refuted Judas by affirming the kind of love Mary showed: one can love both Jesus and the poor: "Then said Jesus, Let her alone: against the day of my burying hath she kept this. For the poor always ye have with you; but me ye have not always."[19] The Joseph Smith Translation (JST) adds to the story: "Then said Jesus, Let her alone: *for she hath preserved this ointment until now, that she might anoint me in token of my burial.*"[20]

It has been assumed that the woman did not know what she was doing and that Jesus, knowing beforehand all things that would befall him, interprets her actions for her and those present. But the text does not necessarily justify such an understanding. It could be understood that the woman anointed him "in anticipation of the burial," meaning that she also knew Jesus' fate.[21]

As on the former occasion when Martha wanted Mary's help in the kitchen, Jesus protected her. As then, he took her as she was and interpreted her extravagant actions as love that would go with him to his death. In any case, Jesus clearly rebuked those present for assuming that their spiritual understanding was greater than that of this woman, and showed them that in this case, the opposite was in fact true.

The anointing precedes three crucial parts of the remainder of the Gospel of John. First, as Jesus' words to Judas suggest, the anointing anticipated Jesus' death and burial, since one did not normally anoint the feet of a living person but rather the feet of the deceased as part of the custom of preparing the whole body for burial. Second, Mary's anointing of Jesus' feet anticipated the washing of feet, which has several meanings.[22] One meaning is very familiar: foot washing is a model of service and discipleship.

Third, Mary's anointing of Jesus anticipated the love commandment that Jesus would give his disciples: "A new commandment I give unto you, that ye love one another; as I have loved you, that ye also love one another. By this shall all men know that ye are my disciples, if ye have love one to another."[23]

One aspect of the anointing story, so important in both Mark and Matthew, is missing from John—Jesus' bold and far-reaching declaration: "Verily I say unto you, wheresoever this gospel shall be preached throughout the whole world, this also that she hath done shall be spoken of for a memorial of her."[24] The Joseph Smith Translation (JST) emphasizes this point by the double repetition of the theme: "For verily she has come beforehand to anoint my body to the burying. She has done what she could: *and this which she has done unto me, shall be had in remembrance in generations to come, wheresoever my gospel shall be preached*; Verily I say unto you, Wheresoever this gospel shall be preached throughout the whole world, what she hath done shall be spoken of also for a memorial of her."[25]

This important theme's absence in John may be explained by the fact that John used a symbol to obtain the same effect—the statement "and the house was filled with the odour of the ointment."[26] According to a well-known rabbinical saying that John may have known, the aroma of perfume is likened to the knowledge of a good name, "[The scent of] good oil is diffused from the bed-chamber to the dining-hall while a good name is diffused from one end of the world to the other."[27] This act of anointing Jesus and the effect of the fragrance filling the entire house can be compared to Mary's good name being spread from one end of the world to the other. That this was the case for the early Church is demonstrated by how Mary is introduced earlier in John 11: "It was that Mary which anointed the Lord with ointment, and wiped his feet with her hair, whose brother Lazarus was sick."[28]

Despite any difference between Mark, Luke, and John, all three Gospels reflect the same basic story: a woman anoints Jesus. The incident causes objections, which Jesus rejects by approving of the woman's action. While John speaks of the anointing of the feet, Mark and Matthew speak of the anointing of the head.[29] Is it possible that she anointed both his head and feet? Since in the Old

Testament, prophets anointed the head of the Jewish king, the anointing of Jesus' head may be seen as the prophetic recognition of Jesus as the Anointed (*Messiah* in English is equivalent to the Hebrew, and *Christ* in English is equivalent to the Greek for "anointed").[30]

Peter had already confessed, without understanding the implications of Jesus' calling, "you are the anointed one"; however, this woman's anointing of Jesus clearly recognized that Jesus' messiahship meant suffering and death, not the overthrow of Roman rule and kingly glory that many Jews anticipated. Instead, Jesus' mission was one of loving service, like the woman who anointed him. Often ignored, forgotten, or simply overshadowed, Mary's role as the one who anointed Jesus at Bethany is significant. The particular prophetic act ascribed to her is also important for another reason. Because the story is placed at a crucial juncture, we are forced to take Mary seriously, not only as a person but also as a vehicle.

Three Unnamed Women (Matthew 26:69–72; 27:19; Mark 14:16–72; Luke 22:56–62)

Two unnamed women appear during Jesus' interrogation before Jewish leaders. Both a "damsel [servant girl]" and a "maid" confronted Peter with the truth that he was Jesus' disciple, which he denied vehemently.[31]

During the trial, only one person interceded to stop the proceeding—again it was a woman. Preserved only in Matthew's Gospel is the story of Pilate's wife. She, like Joseph and the wise men, was warned in a dream that Jesus was a just man [a righteous man]: "When he was set down on the judgment seat, his wife sent unto him, saying, Have thou nothing to do with that *just man*: for I have suffered many things this day in a dream because of him."[32]

The Remaining Women (Matthew 27:55–61; Mark 15:40–47; Luke 23:49–56; John 19:25–27)

During the last week of Jesus' ministry (Jesus' last fateful hours among his disciples), women are depicted as aware, sympathetic, and loyal to his impending call to suffer and die as the servant mentioned in Isaiah 53—the suffering Messiah. Herein we see the effect of Jesus' teachings and life on these women; in the face of death we see the loyalty with which they responded.

The many women at the cross and burial confirmed the contrast between themselves and some of the disciples who deserted Jesus.[33] Certainly they were in as much danger as the men (the Romans customarily killed the family and servants of political criminals). The small group of weeping but none-the-less brave women stood "afar off," not out of trepidation but because the place of execution was cordoned off by the military. Like Mary of Bethany, they acted as disciples offering service to Jesus.

All these examples prepare us to examine the last days of Jesus' life—the passion and the resurrection narrative in which women play a significant role as witnesses.

The Last to Remain, the First to Return and Remember: Women as Witnesses

$\int$tripped of all clothing in an ultimate act of humiliation, Jesus was executed by the horribly cruel method of Roman crucifixion—a most extreme form of punishment reserved for slaves, dangerous and violent criminals, and political enemies of Rome. With faithful women watching, Jesus died an agonizing and painful death.

Though the accounts of the four Gospels differ in many respects in their treatment of Jesus' last hours and subsequent events, all four concur that women were present at the cross and that in the early morning hours of the first day following the Sabbath, women went to Jesus' tomb. They were, according to the four Gospel writers, the first to discover that the tomb was empty and thus were the first to learn of Jesus' resurrection. According to both Mark and John, not only is a woman, Mary Magdalene, the first to discover the empty tomb, she is also the first to see and speak with the risen Christ, who instructs her to go and tell the other disciples.

The Resurrection According to Luke (Luke 23–24)

Luke's story of Jesus' burial and resurrection follows a particular line.[1] When the Lord's body was taken from the cross, Joseph of Arimathaea "wrapped it in linen," a common burial cloth of the period, made of flax from either Egypt or Jericho.[2] The body was then taken to a new tomb, "hewn in stone, wherein never man before was laid."[3] Luke continues, "and the women also, which came with him from Galilee, followed after, and beheld the sepulchre, and how his body was laid. And they returned, and prepared spices and ointments; and rested the sabbath day according to the commandment."[4] In this way the Gospel writers identify the traditional roles women played in taking care of the dead (and thus making themselves ritually impure).

The testimony of those who remained becomes important for Luke's purposes. These faithful disciples actually saw Jesus' dead body placed in the tomb and noted how it was laid. They did so because they wanted to return and offer their final act of devotion to Jesus by anointing his body. However, when they returned, they found the tomb empty.

"Now upon the first day of the week [the Jewish days of the week were simply known as the first, second, third, fourth, fifth, sixth day, and *Shabbat*—Sabbath], very early in the morning, they came unto the sepulchre, bringing the spices which they had prepared, and certain others with them. And they found the stone rolled away from the sepulchre. And they entered in, and found not the body of the Lord Jesus."[5]

Arriving early in the morning was part of the mourning ritual that usually consisted of not eating (fasting), inability to sleep (keeping vigil), unconcern about clothing (wearing sackcloth), and unconcern about appearance (showing unkempt hair and a dirty face, both indicated by ashes on the head).

Unlike the accounts of Matthew and Mark, who mention the women's names three times to emphasize their importance (especially Mary Magdalene), Luke mentions no names at first.[6] Anonymously they came to anoint Jesus' body.[7] Luke furnishes their names only at the end when he notes that Mary Magdalene and the others were among those who told the Apostles about the empty tomb and the vision of angels.

Surely these women were perplexed as they entered the tomb and found it empty. The angels chided them, and when the women reported their discovery, the Apostles thought "their words seemed to them as idle tales, and they believed them not."[8] Nothing in these Apostles' Jewish culture could have prepared them for the testimony of these women, a culture where women could not be witnesses.[9] Remember, generally a woman's testimony, along with that of slaves, was not admissible evidence in court, unless it dealt with a "woman's issue."

As we have already stated, the reason for this, according to Josephus, was "on account of the levity and boldness of their sex."[10] Finally, when Peter came to the tomb, he walked away "wondering."[11]

The women's perplexity seems to have lifted with the revealing words of the angels: "And as they were afraid, and bowed down their faces to the earth, they said unto them, Why seek ye the living among the dead? He is not here, but is risen: remember how he spake unto you when he was yet in Galilee, Saying, The Son of man must be delivered into the hands of sinful men, and be crucified, and the third day rise again. And they remembered his words."[12]

Nothing in the text indicates that their confusion continued after the revelation and explanation. The observation, "and they remembered his words," coming on the heels of the angelic disclosure and explanation, implies understanding in the light of Jesus' prophecy and of what had transpired at the tomb.[13]

The two phrases, "Remember how he spake unto you when he was yet in Galilee" and "they remembered his words," are a key theme of the story.[14] The women, especially Mary Magdalene, have heroines' roles as the first to remember (recall) Jesus' words when he spoke about his pending suffering and death in the divine plan, and the first to grasp their fulfillment.[15]

Luke had already identified these women as companion travelers with Jesus.[16] Luke is careful to identify them *before* Jesus makes his first prediction of his death to his disciples.[17]

This is emphasized, in deliberate contrast to Mark's account, that the women reported "all these things unto the eleven, and to all the rest."[18] The expression "all these things" refers to their total experience—to the empty tomb and to the angelic words. The women reported what they had witnessed and what they had heard. Luke, in effect, strengthens their witnessing by his delayed mentioning of their names until after their report to the disciples.[19] This is meant to underscore their role as eyewitnesses of Jesus' death and burial, of the empty tomb, and of the angelic revelation.[20] Their testimony was clearly important to Luke and the early Church.

In view of the empty tomb, the heavenly testimony of the two angels, and Jesus' previous prophecy of his resurrection, the women now have enough light to understand, seemingly for the

first time, that Jesus had to suffer and die and that he rose from
the dead in fulfillment of his own words. Previously, Jesus' instructions on these points were always met with lack of understanding by the disciples.[21]

The Road to Emmaus (Luke 24:13–35)

The "eleven" and "all the rest" remain incredulous. According to Luke, the next event is the appearance of Jesus to two disciples.[22] As the two walked "to a village called Emmaus, which
was from Jerusalem about three-score furlongs [about seven
miles]," Jesus "drew near, and went with them."[23] That these two
travelers are men is nowhere stated explicitly in the text. Again,
the Jewish witness model (and possibly our own way of looking at
the New Testament) obscures the fact that for Jesus, women can
and do act as legitimate witnesses of these events.

It is therefore not necessary to assume that both travelers were
men. One is named and clearly male, one unnamed and probably
female.[24] The couple may be returning home to Emmaus that day,
for when they arrived they invited Jesus to have dinner with them
in their home.[25]

The two travelers heard the women's report, including their
account of the angels. They had also heard that some of the disciples had verified that the tomb was indeed empty. Yet the two
were now leaving Jerusalem and the assembled disciples. They
were dejected and despondent, as the first part of their dialogue
with Jesus indicates.[26]

Their recognition of the risen Lord is an essential aspect of the
story. The two travelers at first failed to recognize Jesus.[27] They
expressed their lack of understanding of Jesus' identity and mission and their loss of hope because of Jesus' crucifixion, despite
the women's report of "a vision of angels which said that he was
alive."[28] Their failure to recognize him was probably caused by
their lack of insight into God's purpose as attested in scripture and
now realized in Jesus' suffering, death, and resurrection.

The couple's lack of insight was emphasized in that the title
"Christ" was missing from their summary description of Jesus'
identity, activity, and mission. The phrase "to redeem Israel" was

pointedly present in the unknown traveler's response, however.[29] Equally absent was any reference to Jesus' prediction of his death and resurrection. This was underscored by Jesus' response: "O fools, and slow of heart to believe all that the prophets have spoken: Ought not Christ to have suffered these things, and to enter into his glory?"[30]

What restrained these disciples from believing was their poor understanding of the scriptural witnesses to the Resurrection events. The Hebrew scriptures should have prepared them for suffering, death, and resurrection. Jesus then opened the scriptures to them:

> And beginning at Moses and all the prophets, he expounded unto them in all the scriptures the things concerning himself.
> And they drew nigh unto the village, whither they went: and he made as though he would have gone further.
> But they constrained him, saying, Abide with us: for it is toward evening, and the day is far spent. And he went in to tarry with them.
> And it came to pass, as he sat at meat with them, he took bread, and blessed it, and brake, and gave to them.
> And their eyes were opened, and they knew him; and he vanished out of their sight.[31]

Their initial sadness gave way to joy as they eagerly listened to Jesus' explanation of the scriptures. Moreover, their "eyes were opened" at the breaking of bread, and "they knew [recognized] him" when once again he served the meal to them as of old.[32] "And they said one to another, Did not our hearts burn within us, while he talked with us by the way, and while he opened to us the scriptures?"[33] They heard, understood, and accepted this disclosure, and at the meal they recognized Jesus in their midst. Their dejection at leaving Jerusalem was reversed; the two had become harbingers of a joyful message.

"And they rose up the same hour, and returned to Jerusalem, and found the eleven gathered together, and them that were with them, saying, The Lord is risen indeed, and hath appeared to Simon. And they told what things were done in the way, and how he was known of them in breaking of bread."[34]

When they entered the place of gathering, a twist in the

expected conclusion of the narrative was found. Before the two had a chance to tell the assembly in Jerusalem what had happened to them on the road, this gathering of disciples proclaimed to the two that "the Lord is risen indeed, and hath appeared to Simon."[35] The assembly of disciples here proclaimed Jesus' resurrection solely on the basis of his appearance to Peter (a man), independent of the Emmaus event or of the women's earlier testimony. This declaration reversed their former attitude toward the testimony of the women (not believing it originally) as implied in the word *indeed* (really).

The testimony of these two travelers, the latest development reported to them, corroborated what the entire congregation now knew and believed. Several independent witnesses, both men and women, now emerged among the followers of Jesus.

Jesus Appears to the Eleven (Luke 24:36–48)

It is possible that the Eleven and "them that were with them" were gathered in the very same upper room where Jesus spent his last night with the Twelve.[36] If this upper room was the same place, it might have been the home of another important female disciple, the mother of John Mark:[37]

> And as they thus spake, Jesus himself stood in the midst of them, and saith unto them, Peace be unto you.
>
> But they were terrified and afrighted, and supposed that they had seen a spirit.
>
> And he said unto them, Why are ye troubled? and why do thoughts arise in your hearts?
>
> Behold my hands and my feet, that it is I myself: handle me, and see; for a spirit hath not flesh and bones, as ye see me have.
>
> And when he had thus spoken, he shewed them his hands and his feet.[38]

Our picture of this gathering must be enlarged to include not only the Eleven but also "them that were with them," probably including both women and men.[39] Jesus invites the disciples, including any women present, to see and touch him.[40]

The Resurrection According to Matthew (Matthew 28)

Matthew adds one special detail about Jesus' death that explains how the huge stone was rolled away for the women who came to visit the tomb.

"And behold, the veil of the temple was rent in twain from the top to the bottom; *and the earth did quake, and the rocks rent.*"[41] Only Matthew tells of an "aftershock" occurring on the third day, "And behold, *there was a great earthquake*: for the angel of the Lord descended from heaven, and came and rolled back the stone from the door, and sat upon it."[42]

Matthew also indicates that the women joyfully ran from the empty tomb in order to tell the disciples the good news. Subsequently they encountered the risen Jesus, who likewise entrusted to them the task of announcing the good news of his resurrection.[43]

"And they departed quickly from the sepulchre with fear and great joy; and did run to bring his disciples word. And as they went to tell his disciples, behold, Jesus met them, saying, All hail. And they came and held him by the feet, and worshipped him. Then said Jesus unto them, Be not afraid: go tell my brethren that they go into Galilee, and there shall they see me."[44]

The Resurrection According to Mark (Mark 16)

Mark clearly identified the women, especially Mary Magdalene, as being present at the tomb during the early morning hours: "When the sabbath was past, Mary Magdalene, and Mary the mother of James, and Salome, had bought sweet spices, that they might come and anoint him."[45] They confirmed that the angels commissioned the women to be the real heralds of the resurrection to the Twelve. In Matthew, Mark, and Luke, without the women there would have been no witnesses to Jesus' death, burial, empty tomb, and resurrection. Jesus did not die alone.

Mark emphasized that the disciples did not give credence to the words of the women concerning the resurrection: "Afterward he appeared unto the eleven as they sat at meat, and upbraided them with their unbelief and hardness of heart, because they believed not them which had seen him after he was risen."[46] That the news had come via women was obviously no excuse for their "unbelief and hardness of heart."

The Resurrection According to John (John 20:1–18)

John's Gospel clearly differs from that of Matthew, Mark, and Luke. The story of Mary Magdalene and the risen Christ as told by John was the most detailed about the women at Jesus' tomb. John divided the story into two separate scenes: Mary at the empty tomb, and Mary with the risen Christ.[47]

On the first day of the Jewish week, Mary arrived at Jesus' tomb only to find the stone rolled away from its opening. According to the Gospel of John, Mary Magdalene ran back within the city walls to tell Peter and the disciples that the master's body was missing. She offered the only logical explanation, "They have taken away the Lord out of the sepulchre."[48] The preresurrection world could not make sense of an empty tomb. The only acceptable explanation could be graverobbing. Peter, the beloved disciple (John), and Mary returned to the site, but Peter and John returned to "their own home" once they examined the tomb.

The second scene begins as "Mary stood without at the sepulchre weeping."[49] Puzzled and dazed at not finding Jesus' body, Mary bent down again to look inside the tomb. Mary then conversed with two white-robed messengers at the head and foot of the place where Jesus' body had been laid. They said to her, "Woman, why weepest thou?"[50] She replied, "Because they have taken away my Lord, and I know not where they have laid him."[51] Her words were more personal here than her first report to Peter and John, for she refers to the Christ as "*my* Lord," instead of "*the* Lord," and she said, "*I* know not where they have laid him," instead of "*we* know not where they have laid him."[52]

Mary then turned towards the garden, and "she saw the resurrected Christ not knowing it was him." The first words of the risen Jesus are a series of questions that he asks Mary, "Woman, why weepest thou? whom seekest thou?"[53]

At the beginning of his Gospel, John preserves Jesus' words to the disciples of John the Baptist as they approach him. "Then Jesus turned, and saw them following, and saith unto them, What seek ye?"[54] This question is an invitation that introduces one of the marks of discipleship in John—to look for Jesus. The repetition of that question, "What seek ye?" in the resurrection narrative establishes continuity between the first disciples and Mary.

"She, supposing him to be the gardener, saith unto him, Sir, if thou have borne him hence, tell me where thou hast laid him, and I will take him away."[55] John employs this threefold repetition of Mary Magdalene's words to describe her ardent longing to find Jesus whom she loved so much.

Later rabbinic tradition referred to the human corpse as the "father of the fathers of uncleanness." Persons and objects polluted by coming in direct contact with a corpse were impure for seven days. Pollution occured when the persons or objects touched the corpse or were merely in the same enclosure with it.[56] Mary, with a total disregard for Mosaic regulations, wanted to find Jesus' body herself and planned to "take him away" if necessary.

The "gardener" then changed Mary's life forever when he called her by name: "Mary." She turned around again, but this time she saw Jesus, her Master.

"She turned herself, and saith unto him, Rabboni; which is to say, Master. Jesus saith unto her, Touch me not; for I am not yet ascended to my Father: but go to my brethren, and say unto them, I ascend unto my Father, and your Father; and to my God, and your God."[57]

Mary did not recognize Jesus until he called her by name. Being called personally by Jesus is a special privilege in John's Gospel. In the parable of the good shepherd, Jesus said, "[The shepherd] calleth his own sheep by name."[58] The "sheep follow him: for they know his voice."[59] Jesus called Lazarus by name to summon him from the tomb, and now his voice summoned Mary to a new reality—the tomb was empty, and life was restored.[60]

John highlights the encounter between Mary and the risen Lord by noting the exact word that Mary would use in Aramaic, *Rabboni.* "Lord, Master" is a literal rendering of *rabboni* rather than teacher or master in this case. Mary knew that this was the risen Lord, not just her teacher.[61]

Mary may have embraced Jesus after she recognized him, because he said to her, "Do not hold on to me," in the Greek, or "Hold me not" in the Joseph Smith Translation (JST),[62] both of which potentially imply that she was already touching him when Jesus spoke to her. This was not a harsh rebuke; rather, it was the first postresurrection teaching. Jesus' prohibition was followed by a positive exhortation, "But go to my brethren, and say unto them, I ascend unto my Father, and your Father; and to my God, and your God."[63]

Mary fulfilled Messianic scripture when she heeded Jesus' words and went to the disciples with the announcement, "I have seen the Lord."[64] In Psalms we find, "I will declare *thy name* unto *my brethren*, in the midst of the congregation will I praise thee."[65] It must be remembered that the Greek word for Lord (*kyrios*) is the same word rendered in the Greek Old Testament (Septuagent) for the tetragrammaton, *YHWH* (Jehovah), which is the proper name of God.[66]

Mary Magdalene became an "apostle to the Apostles." The term does not mean a member of the Twelve (the more significant title) but rather that she is "one sent forth" to witness the good news of the Christ's resurrection.[67] Mary Magdalene was the first witness of the resurrection in two important and significant ways. She was the first person to see the resurrected Messiah, and she was the first person to witness to others what she had seen. She was in a sense the first disciple of the risen Jesus.

Chapter Fourteen

Neither Male nor Female:
One in Christ Jesus

The prominence of women in the early Christian Church has long been acknowledged.[1] It was recognized as such by both the early Christian writers and their opponents.[2] When the pagan critic Celsus denigrated Christianity in the second century as a religion of women, children, and slaves, he articulated a connection between women and early Christianity that has only recently received serious attention.[3] By his equating Christianity with women, children, and slaves, Celsus may have meant merely to confirm what elite, educated men in the Roman world already believed: any religion that appealed to women was the wrong sort of religion.

According to the four Gospels, Jesus' relations with women seem to have been remarkably open, given the reserve that Jewish culture and customs in his day required. It is certain that some of these women did not conform to the most socially acceptable categories of virgin daughter, respectable wife, and mother of legitimate children. Frequently, they were anomalous not merely by virtue of their gender but also by additional marginal conditions specific to women.

For example, many were unmarried or widowed. Jesus broke down barriers in the most surprising ways. Social customs, especially those termed in religious language of first-century rabbinic Judaism, were rejected. As Jesus met women during his ministry, he dealt with them as individuals. When he encountered the woman taken in adultery, for example, he did not ignore the fact that she was a sinner. Rather he acknowledged it and took the opportunity to call her to a new life. She was held accountable for her own failings but was taught to create a new heart with forgiveness from God. In this way, Jesus treated women and men alike.

Each could communicate with Jesus, follow him, be companions with him, minister to him, be ministered by him, and love him. Regardless of the fact that Jesus was a male, the four Gospels demonstrate that even in everyday life women and men could relate to him in the same way, and he related to them in the same way.

The disciples who wrote the four New Testament Gospels (preserving Jesus' words and deeds) not only retell the stories in a matter-of-fact way but also openly reveal their own reactions to Jesus' actions. Jesus challenged the cultural norms of his day by teaching women and calling them forward to discipleship. In the end, a woman's qualification for discipleship was the same as a man's: all must accept him as their Lord and Master. Any person who truly accepts him consequently becomes a witness of him as the source of Living Water.

On one occasion, Jesus saw the crowds of people worried and dejected. "But when he saw the multitudes, he was moved with compassion on them, because they fainted, and were scattered abroad, as sheep having no shepherd. . . . The harvest truly is plenteous, but the labourers are few."[4] So, Jesus commanded the disciples to pray to the "Lord of the harvest, that he will send forth labourers into his harvest."[5] Even when seventy (or seventy-two) more were sent forth, Jesus continued to command the disciples to pray for more laborers.[6] Among those sent were faithful women, as can be seen in the book of Acts and the Epistles.

In Luke's book of Acts, we read that the first group of Christian faithful included "women, and Mary the mother of Jesus."[7] From this small beginning the members of "The Way," as the early Christians were known by nonbelievers, spread their message of hope and salvation throughout the known Mediterranean world.[8]

This message was profoundly and radically challenging to Greco-Roman values and ideas. For Jesus, marriage was indissoluble. Yet divorce was common and had been allowed since the moorings of Greco-Roman culture were established. Another principle that Jesus preached that Romans found disturbing was that men and women had equal dignity in marriage. That these fundamental ideas contributed no small amount to giving Christian women a new consciousness and to teaching Christian men

greater respect for women is beyond dispute. As a result, men and women were more equally yoked, giving both more purpose in life and more happiness in its living.

The new tradition of female equality established by Jesus was transmitted to the early Christian Saints. They attempted to fulfill their master's command to preach the good news to every creature. As missionaries were sent forth and congregations of the faithful were organized, Jesus' words and deeds were remembered. The stories of the "women who followed Jesus" were remembered and the lessons learned. Together the men and women of the early Church began to see that Jesus not only questioned the religious traditions of a fallen world but also challenged the false social, economic, and political ideas of mankind—including those false notions about the role of women.

The Saints of God learned that a woman was not less because she was a female and not meritorious only if she was married and biologically capable of bearing children. Rather, her intrinsic worth was based on being a divine creation of God Almighty. Jesus did not judge anyone by contemporary artificial economic, social, or gender categories. New Testament women did, however, find value in their individual worth as women and as followers of Jesus.

As we now view these women of the four Gospels, sisters at the well—thirsty and weary, burdened with care and tradition, dropping their leather buckets into the well and drawing up unto themselves refreshment and strength—the parched ground bears fruit, and they turn to us with their clay jars filled with water. They witness to us of its goodness, through their model of discipleship, joining hands with the good men they served with. Although Jesus (and therefore the Gospel writers) in no way sought to deny or diminish the distinction between men and women, he emphasized their partnership; it is therefore difficult to find differences in Jesus' approach to women and to men.

Earlier we quoted a prayer that was recited daily by devote Jewish men: "Blessed art thou . . . who hast not made me a heathen [Gentile] . . . who hast not made me a woman. . . who hast not made me a slave."[9] This prayer was reworded and negated by one of Jesus' disciples in the book of Galatians:

> For ye are all the children of God by faith in Christ Jesus.
>
> For as many of you as have been baptized into Christ have put on Christ.
>
> There is neither Jew nor Greek, there is neither bond nor free, there is neither male nor female: for ye are all one in Christ Jesus.
>
> And if ye be Christ's then are ye Abraham's seed, and heirs according to the promise.[10]

Notes

Introduction

1. John 20:15; 21:15–17.
2. Matthew 16:21–22.
3. Mark 14:9; see also Matthew 26:13.

Chapter 1. Sisters at the Well

1. John 4:5–7.
2. Thus, when Jesus later told his disciples to follow a man "bearing a pitcher of water" from a well in order to be properly guided to a room for their Passover celebration, it was noteworthy, for normally a man would never do this chore; see Mark 14:13.
3. Genesis 24:11.
4. Genesis 29:1–2, 9.
5. Exodus 2:15–16.
6. See Genesis 33:18–19; John 4:5–6.
7. John 4:9.
8. See David Daube, "Jesus and the Samaritan Woman: The Meaning of *synchraomai,*" *Journal of Biblical Literature* 69 (1950): 137–47.
9. John 4:27.
10. See John 4:11, 15, 19.
11. *Kyrie* is the vocative of *kyrios* (Lord); see Max Zerwick and

Mary Grosvenor, *A Grammatical Analysis of the Greek New Testament* (Rome: Biblical Institute Press, 1981), p. 295.

12. John 4:11–12; italics added.

13. John 4:13–14.

14. John 4:15; italics added.

15. John 4:16–19; italics added.

16. John 4:20–26.

17. John 4:28–29.

18. John 4:30, 39.

Chapter 2. The Daughters of Pandora and Eve

1. An introductory survey is Pauline Schmitt Pantel, ed., *A History of Women in the West: From Ancient Goddesses to Christian Saints* (Cambridge, Massachusetts: Belknap Press of Harvard University Press, 1992).

2. Hesiod, *Theogony*, lines 550–601; see Hesiod, *Theogony, Works and Days, Shield,* trans. Apostolos N. Athanassakis (Baltimore: Johns Hopkins University Press, 1983), pp. 27–28.

3. Aristotle, *Generation of Animals*, II.iii; see Aristotle, *Generation of Animals*, trans. A.L. Peck (Cambridge: Harvard University Press, 1953), p. 175.

4. Sophocles, *Ajax*, line 293; see *The Complete Greek Tragedies*, ed. David Grene and Richmond Lattimore, 2 vols. (Chicago: University of Chicago Press, 1959), 2:224.

5. See Grace Macurdy, *Hellenistic Queens* (Baltimore: John Hopkins University Press, 1932), and W. W. Tarn and G. T. Griffith, *Hellenistic Civilization* (London: Arnold, 1952).

6. See Judith P. Hallett, "The Role of Women in Roman Elegy: Counter-Cultural Feminism," *Arethusa* 6 (1973):103–24.

7. Marcus Tullins Cicero, *Pro Murena*, XXII. xxvii; see Cicero, *The Speeches*, trans. Lewis Lord, (Cambridge: Harvard University Press, 1959), pp. 179–80.

8. Demosthenes, *Orations: Against Neaera* LIX.122; see *Demosthenes*, trans. A. T. Murray, 3 vols. (Cambridge: Harvard University Press, 1958), 3:445, 447.

9. See for example the plight of Psecas, a slave in a Roman household, Jo-Ann Shelton, *As the Romans Did: A Source Book in*

Roman Social History (New York: Oxford University Press, 1988), pp. 177–78.

10. See Paul Veyne, ed., *A History of Private Life: From Pagan Rome to Byzantium* (Cambridge: Belknap Press of Harvard University Press, 1987), pp. 202–5.

11. For example, actresses sometimes appeared nude and even performed sexual acts on stage.

12. Such artwork seems to indicate that many forms of sexual acts between humans, as well as acts between humans and animals, were accepted and practiced.

13. Posidippus, *Hermaphr;* as cited in Eva Cantarella, *Pandora's Daughters: The Role and Status of Women in Greek and Roman Antiquity* (Baltimore: Johns Hopkins University Press, 1987), p. 44.

14. C. Plinius Caecilius Secundus, *Epistularum* VI. xxiv; see *Pliny: Letters*, trans. William Melmoth, rev. W.M.L. Hutchinson, 2 vols. (Cambridge: Harvard University Press, 1961), 1:507.

15. ILS 8043 Rome (2nd century B.C.) inscription as quoted in Michael Massey, *Women in Ancient Greece and Rome* (Cambridge: Cambridge University Press, 1988), p. 21.

16. See Shaye J. D. Cohen, *From the Maccabees to the Mishnah* (Philadelphia: Westminster Press, 1987); John Riches, *The World of Jesus: First-Century Judaism in Crisis* (New York: Cambridge University Press, 1990); and E.P. Sanders, *Judaism: Practice and Belief 63 BCE–66 CE* (Philadelphia: Trinity Press International, 1992).

17. See Stephen E. Robinson, "The Setting of the Gospels," in *Studies in Scripture: Volume Five, The Gospel* (Salt Lake City: Deseret Book Co., 1986), pp. 10–37; particularly his discussion of "Religious Diversity," pp. 22–29.

18. See "Pentateuch," Bible Dictionary, LDS Edition of the King James Version of the Bible (Salt Lake City: The Church of Jesus Christ of Latter-day Saints, 1979), p. 748.

19. The Essenes at Qumran accused the Pharisees of being too lenient in their practice of the Law—"seekers of smooth things," as the Pharisees were called. This was apparently a pun for "seekers of correct behavior," *dorshe ha-hlakhot*—a good description of the Pharisees, but by changing two letters those at Qumran could call them *dorshe ha-halaqot*—"seekers of smooth things"; see E. P.

Sanders, *Judaism: Practice and Belief, 63 BCE–66 CE* (Philadelphia: Trinity Press International, 1992), p. 532, n. 1.

20. See William Whiston, trans., *Josephus: Complete Works* (Grand Rapids, Michigan: Kregel Publications, 1972).

21. See Herbert Danby, trans., *The Mishnah: Translated from the Hebrew with Introduction and Brief Explanatory Notes* (London: Oxford University Press, 1974); I. Epstein, ed., *Hebrew-English Edition of the Babylonian Talmud,* 25 vols. (London: Soncino Press, 1989); and H. Freedman and Maurice Simon, ed., *Midrash Rabbah,* 10 vols. (London: Soncino Press, 1951).

22. See Theodor H. Gaster, trans., *The Dead Sea Scriptures* (New York: Anchor Books, 1976) and Yigael Yadin, ed., *The Temple Scroll,* 3 vols. (Jerusalem: The Israel Exploration Society, 1983).

23. See James H. Charlesworth, ed., *The Old Testament Pseudepigrapha,* 2 vols. (Garden City, New York: Doubleday & Company, Inc., 1983–85).

24. Unless otherwise noted, all biblical citations come from the King James Version (KJV) of the Bible. The earliest translation of the Bible was the Greek Septuagint (ca. 285 B.C.), frequently abbreviated LXX; *The Septuagint with Apocrypha: Greek and English,* trans. Sir Lancelot C. L. Brenton (1851; reprint, Grand Rapids, Michigan: Zondervan Publishing House, 1975). Sometime thereafter, Aramaic translations appeared in Jewish Palestine in use by Jesus' time; see for example *The Aramaic Bible: Targum Onqelos to Leviticus and Numbers* (Wilmington, Delaware: Michael Glazier, Inc., 1988).

25. See Judith Baskin, "The Separation of Women in Rabbinic Judaism," in Ellison Findly and Yvonne Haddad, eds., *Women, Religion and Social Change* (Albany: Statute University of New York Press, 1984), pp. 3–18.

26. An interpretation of a woman's status in these documents is Claudia V. Camp, "Understanding a Patriarchy: Women in Second Century [B.C.] Jerusalem through the Eyes of Ben Sira," in Amy-Jill Levine, ed., *"Women Like This": New Perspectives on Jewish Women in the Greco-Roman World* (Atlanta: Scholars Press, 1991), pp. 1–39.

27. *Temple Scroll,* col. xlvi; see Yigael Yadin, ed., *The Temple Scroll,* 1:305–7.

28. See "Phylacteries," Bible Dictionary, LDS Edition of the KJV, p. 751.

29. *Mishnah,* Sotah 3.4; see Herbert Danby, trans., *The Mishnah,* p. 296.

30. *Mishnah,* Aboth 1.5; see Herbert Danby, trans. *The Mishnah,* p. 446.

31. Flavius Josephus, *Jewish Antiquities* IV. 219; see William Whiston, trans., *Josephus: Complete Works,* p. 97.

32. See Exodus 15:20; Judges 4–5; and 2 Kings 22:14–20.

33. Yet even these remarkable women of Judaism were often identified with less than desirable qualities. "Women are said to possess four traits," a rabbinical commentary stated, "they are greedy, eavesdroppers, slothful, and envious." Eve, Sarah, Rachel, and Miriam were used to demonstrate the rabbi's position; see *Midrash Rabbah,* Genesis, XLV.5; see H. Freedman and Maurice Simon, eds., *Midrash Rabbah,* 1:383.

34. Flavius Josephus, *Against Apion* II, 202; see William Whiston, trans., *Josephus: Complete Works,* p. 632.

35. *Babylonian Talmud,* Menahoth 43b; see *Tractate Menahoth* 43b, volume 23 in I. Epstein, ed., *Hebrew-English Edition of the Babylonian Talmud.*

36. Attributed to Plato or Thales, as quoted in Wayne A. Meeks, "The Image of the Androgyne: Some Uses of a Symbol in Earliest Christianity," *History of Religions,* vol. 13, no. 3 (February 1974):167.

Chapter 3. A Woman's World

1. Jacob Neusner, "How Judaism and Christianity Can Talk to Each Other," *Bible Review* 6 (December 1990):36.

2. 1 Nephi 13:24–28.

3. These rules are found in the "covenant code" (Exodus 20:22–23:33) regarding selling one's daughter into slavery; "priestly code" (Leviticus 1:1–15:32) regarding purification and uncleanness as a result of childbirth and other "flows of blood"; "holiness code" (Leviticus 17:1–26:46) regarding sexual relations; the laws concerning a woman suspected of adultery (Numbers 5:11–31); laws of inheritance (Numbers 27:1–11; 36:5–12); laws

regarding vows (Numbers 30:1–16); and laws concerning women prisoners of war, dress, adultery, and sexual relations with betrothed women, divorce, levirate marriage, and other miscellaneous activities relating to women (Deuteronomy 5:1–26:19, 28:1–68).

4. Leviticus 12:4.

5. See Leviticus 12:1–8. Mary and Joseph were probably poor since they offered two birds after Jesus' birth; see Luke 2:22–24.

6. Flavius Josephus, *Against Apion* II.202; see William Whiston, trans., *Josephus: Complete Works* (Grand Rapids, Michigan: Kregel Publications, 1972), p. 632.

7. Cornelius Tacitus, *Historiarum* V.v; see Tacitus, *The Histories*, trans. Clifford Moore, 2 vols. (Cambridge: Harvard University Press, 1956), 2:183.

8. See E. P. Sanders, *Jewish Law from Jesus to the Mishnah: Five Studies* (Philadelphia: Fortress Press, 1990), pp. 214–27.

9. *Midrash Rabbah,* Genesis, XVII.2; see H. Freedman and Maurice Simon, eds., *Midrash Rabbah,* 10 vols. (New York: Soncino Press, 1951) 1:132.

10. See for example, Gordon J. Wenham, "Betulah: A Girl of Marriageable Age," *Vetus Testamentum* 22 (July 1972):326–48.

11. See Jo-Ann Shelton, *As the Romans Did: A Source Book in Roman Social History* (New York: Oxford University Press, 1988), p. 292.

12. See Deuteronomy 22:13–21.

13. For the reaction of the people to his presence at Capernaum, see Mark 1:22.

Chapter 4. Separate Witnesses

1. Synopsis is from the Greek *synoptos,* "that can be seen at a glance, in full view"; Liddell and Scott, *An Intermediate Greek-English Lexicon* (Oxford: Clarendon Press, 1975), p. 779.

2. An excellent and accessible harmony is found under "Gospel," Bible Dictionary, in the LDS Edition of the King James Version of the Bible, pp. 684–96. Two related harmonies are Thomas M. Mumford, *Horizontal Harmony of the Four Gospels in Parallel Columns* (Salt Lake City: Deseret Book Co., 1979) and Steven J. Hite and Julie Melville Hite, *The Joseph Smith Translation of the Four Gospels: A Harmony* (Orem, Utah: S & J Publishing, 1989).

3. Walter W. Skeat, *A Concise Etymological Dictionary of the English Language* (Oxford: Clarendon Press, 1976), p. 218.

4. The Greek *euangelion* (good news) was known to secular authors and was used to announce a victory or great events in the life of the emperor. For a more complete discussion of its usage, see William F. Arndt and Wilbur F. Gingrich, *A Greek-English Lexicon of the New Testament and Other Early Christian Literature* (Chicago: University of Chicago Press, 1957), p. 318.

5. Heinrich Greeven in Albert Huck, *Synopse der drei ersten Evangelien/Synopsis of the First Three Gospels with the Addition of the Johannine Parallels* (Tunbingen, W. Germany: J. C. B. Mohr [Paul Siebeck], 1981), xxxvi.

6. Liddell and Scott, *An Intermediate Greek-English Lexicon*, p. 779.

7. See John 13–17.

8. For an excellent introduction to Mark's Gospel from an LDS scholar's perspective, see S. Kent Brown, "The Testimony of Mark," in *Studies in Scripture: Volume Five, The Gospels,* ed. Kent P. Jackson and Robert L. Millet (Salt Lake City: Deseret Book Co., 1986), pp. 61–87.

9. See Acts 12:12, 25; 13:5; 15:36-41; Philemon 1:24; Colossians 4:10; 2 Timothy 4:11 for his association with Paul and Barnabas. Mark is described as "Marcus my son" by Peter (1 Peter 5:13). Eusebius reported an early tradition, that of second-century Papias of Hierapolis, that Mark wrote his Gospel under Peter's direction, "Mark being the interpreter of Peter whatsoever he recorded he wrote with great accuracy," Eusebius, *Ecclesiastical History* 3.39.15; see Eusebius, *Ecclesiastical History* (Grand Rapids, Michigan: Baker Books House, 1991), p. 127. If this is partially accurate, it would explain why some of the stories found in Mark are told simply, with some details suggesting a basis in a Petrine recollection; see for example Mark 1:29–31.

10. Mark 7:3; see also 12:18; 14:12; 15:42.

11. Mark 5:41; see also 3:17; 7:11, 34; 15:22, 34.

12. See Mark 6:19–20; both Matthew and Mark present the unique story of Herod Antipas's birthday party when Herodias's daughter dances for him and requests John the Baptist's head. We know the daughter's name from Josephus, not the New Testament; Flavius Josephus, *Antiquities* XVIII. 136; see William Whiston, trans., *Josephus: Complete Works* (Grand Rapids, Michigan:

Kregel Publications, 1972), p. 383. There is some confusion regarding her first husband. Some scholars believe Mark erroneously calls her the wife of Philip, the tetrarch of Trachonitis (Luke 3:1; see also Matthew 14:6). They conclude that she was actually the wife of Herod Antipas's other brother Herod.

13. Mark 15:40; 16:1

14. See Mark 2:14 and Luke 5:23, but who is called Matthew in the parallel passage in Matthew 9:9.

15. For a discussion of the sources for Matthew's Gospel, see Robert L. Millet, "The Testimony of Matthew," in *Studies in Scripture: Volume Five, The Gospels,* pp. 38–60.

16. See "Septuagint," Bible Dictionary, LDS Edition of the KJV, p. 771.

17. Matthew 14:21.

18. Matthew 15:38.

19. See especially Matthew 23:8–12.

20. Matthew 20:26–27.

21. The women at the cross and tomb (Matthew 27:55–28:61); Herodias and her daughter (Matthew 6:17–28); coming to Jesus for healing (Matthew 5:21–34; 7:24–30); performing loving service (Matthew 14:3–9); examples of faith (Matthew 12:41–44); and speaking the truth (Matthew 14:66-69).

22. For a discussion of sources and time of writing of the Gospel of Luke, see Richard Lloyd Anderson, "The Testimony of Luke," in *Studies in Scripture: Volume Five, The Gospels,* pp. 88–108.

23. Acts 1:1–2.

24. See Luke 1:1–4.

25. Luke 1:45.

26. Luke 18:4.

27. See Luke 2:19; 2:33; 2:50–51.

28. Acts 1:14.

29. Luke 7:11–17.

30. Luke 7:36–50.

31. Luke 13:10–17.

32. See Luke 15:8–10; 18:1–8.

33. For background information and a discussion of themes and ideas found in the Gospel of John, see C. Wilford Griggs, "The Testimony of John," in *Studies in Scripture: Volume Five, The Gospels,* pp. 109–26.

34. John 1:11–12.
35. John 4:4–42; 7:53–8:11; 11:1–44.
36. John 2:1–11.
37. John 12:1–8; 19:25–27; 20:1–18.
38. John 2:1–11; 19:25–27.
39. See John 2:1, 2, 5; 19:25–26; 2:4; 19:26.
40. John 4:1–42.

Chapter 5. The Surprising Five

1. Matthew 1:1; see James B. Bell, *The Roots of Jesus: A Genealogical Investigation* (Garden City, New York: Doubleday & Company, Inc., 1983) and Raymond E. Brown, *The Birth of the Messiah: A Commentary on the Infancy Narratives in Matthew and Luke* (Garden City, New York: Image Books, 1979).

2. See Moses 6:5, 8.

3. When Luke's genealogy of Jesus is compared with Matthew's, one notices several important differences. Matthew, in descending order, lists Jesus' roots from Abraham, while Luke's genealogy ascends from Jesus to David to Abraham through Adam to God. Luke's list of seventy-seven names is therefore longer than Matthew's forty-one. Some have thought that Matthew's record is of Joseph's family while Luke presents Mary's genealogy, or that Matthew's represents the royal genealogy and Luke's presents a personal pedigree; see James E. Talmage, *Jesus the Christ* (Salt Lake City: Deseret Book Co., 1970), pp. 83–90; Bruce R. McConkie, *Doctrinal New Testament Commentary*, 3 vols. (Salt Lake City: Bookcraft, Inc., 1965), 1:94–95.

4. See Genesis 38.

5. See Joshua 2, 6.

6. See Ruth 3.

7. See 2 Samuel 11.

8. See Matthew 1:18–25.

9. Genesis 38:7.

10. Genesis 38:8–10.

11. Genesis 38:11.

12. Genesis 38:14.

13. Genesis 38:16.

14. Genesis 38:17–18.

15. Genesis 38:24.
16. Genesis 38:24.
17. Genesis 38:26.
18. Joshua 2:1.
19. Joshua 2:1.
20. Joshua 2:3.
21. Joshua 2:6.
22. Joshua 2:9–11.
23. Joshua 6:25.
24. See, for example, Ruth 1:22; 2:2, 6, 21.
25. Genesis 19:30–33, 37.
26. See Numbers 22–25; Judges 3:12–30; 11:17; 2 Samuel 8:2; 2 Kings 3:6–27; 13:20; 24:2; 1 Chronicles 18:2; 2 Chronicles 20:1–25.
27. Ruth 3:6–9.
28. Ruth 4:13.
29. 2 Samuel 11:3.
30. 2 Samuel 11:2.
31. 2 Samuel 11:4.
32. JST, Matthew 1:6. For a complete text of the Joseph Smith Translation, see *The Holy Scriptures: Inspired Version* (Independence, Missouri: Herald Publishing House, 1974).
33. 2 Samuel 11:5.
34. 2 Samuel 11:27.
35. 2 Samuel 12:6.
36. 2 Samuel 12:7.
37. 2 Samuel 12:24.
38. Matthew 1:18.
39. Matthew 1:19.
40. Matthew 1:20.
41. Matthew 1:22–23.
42. Luke 3:23–38.
43. Especially the following, Raymond E. Brown, *The Virginal Conception and Bodily Resurrection of Jesus* (New York: Paulist Press, 1973); Raymond E. Brown, Karl P. Donfried, Joseph A. Fitzmyer, John Reumann, *Mary in the New Testament* (Philadelphia: Fortress Press, 1978).
44. Matthew 1:21; italics added.
45. See Raymond E. Brown, *The Birth of the Messiah* (Garden City, New York: Image Books, 1979), pp. 71–74.

46. See Albert Rouet, *A Short Dictionary of the New Testament* (New York: Paulist Press, 1982), p. 73.

47. Mark 6:1–2.

48. Mark 6:2–3.

49. John 8:41.

50. *Babylonian Talmud,* Shabbath 104b; see *Tractate Shabbath,* 104b, volume 3 in I. Epstein, ed., *Hebrew-English Edition of the Babylonian Talmud,* 25 vols. (London: Soncino Press, 1989).

51. 1 Kings 1:17.

Chapter 6. The First Believers

1. Luke 1:5. Herod the Great, the son of the Idumean Antipater, ruled Jewish Palestine from 37 B.C. to 4 B.C. by arrangement with Rome; see L. I. Levine, "Herod the Great," *The Anchor Bible Dictionary,* ed. David Noel Freedman, 6 vols. (New York: Doubleday, 1992), 3:161–69.

2. See Exodus 6:23.

3. Luke 1:6.

4. See Genesis 17:15–21; 18:9–15; 21:1–7; Judges 13:2–5; 1 Samuel 1:1–20.

5. See Genesis 16:1; 17:7.

6. From Luke 1:23, we learn that when Zacharias finished his service in the temple he returned to his own home without telling us where it is, but Luke 1:39 clarified that it was in a town in the hill country of Judaea (ancient Judah). Christian tradition identifies the place as Ain Karim, some five miles west of Jerusalem.

7. Luke 1:43.

8. See Luke 1:45.

9. Luke 1:41–42.

10. Luke 1:41–42.

11. See Luke 1:15.

12. Luke 1:42–45.

13. Luke 1:57–63.

14. Luke 1:26–38; 2:1–21.

15. Luke 1:26–38.

16. Luke 1:26; the lake is called "the sea of Tiberias" in John 6:1.

17. Surprisingly, Sepphoris (the most important city of Galilee, only four miles from Nazareth) and later the new Galilean political

capital of Herod Antipas, Tiberias, Sebaste (the city in Samaria), and Caesarea (the capital of Roman Palestine) are not mentioned. It seems obvious that Jesus' ministry did not take him to cities, except Jerusalem, where the temple was located.

18. See Luke 1:28.

19. Luke 11:27–28.

20. See Matthew 1:20, 24.

21. See Matthew 1:19.

22. Matthew 1:19.

23. Deuteronomy 22:21 specifies stoning as the punishment for unchastity on the part of a betrothed woman, while Leviticus 20:10 simply orders the death penalty for an unfaithful married woman.

24. *Babylonian Talmud,* Sanhedrin 52a; see *Tractate Sandrin* 52a, volume 19 in I. Epstein, ed., *Hebrew-English Edition for the Babylonian Talmud,* 25 vols. (London: Soncino Press, 1989).

25. Matthew 1:20.

26. See Matthew 1:21.

27. Luke 1:26–31.

28. See Genesis 16:11; 30:13; Judges 13:24; 1 Samuel 1:20.

29. JST, Luke 1:28–29; italics added.

30. Luke 1:34.

31. Luke 1:35.

32. Luke 1:38.

33. See Muhammad A. Dandamayev, "Slavery," *The Anchor Bible Dictionary,* 6:62.

34. Matthew 22:27; Acts 2:17–18, citing Joel 2:28–32.

35. Joel 2:28–29; italics added.

36. Luke 1:46–55.

37. Luke 1:42–45.

38. Luke 1:47; 1:49; 1:48.

39. Luke 1:46–55; compare JST, Luke 1:46–55.

40. See 1 Samuel 1:11; 2:1–10.

41. See Psalms 33, 47, 48, 113, 117, 135, and especially 136.

42. See Luke 1:35; Luke 9:34.

43. See Max Zerwick and Mary Grosvenor, *A Grammatical Analysis of the Greek New Testament* (Rome: Biblical Institute Press, 1981), p. 172, and William F. Arndt and F. Wilbur Gingrich, eds., *A Greek-English Lexicon of the New Testament* (Chicago: University of Chicago Press, 1957), p. 298.

44. Luke 1:56.

45. Luke 2:1–5.

46. Luke 2:6–7.

47. Luke 2:7.

48. Mark 14:14; Luke 22:11.

49. The Joseph Smith Translation emphasizes that "this is the way ye shall find the babe"; JST, Luke 2:12.

50. Luke 2:8–12.

51. See Luke 1:18–20; 1:36.

52. Luke 2:16.

53. See Acts 1:6.

54. Luke 2:17–18.

55. Luke 2:19.

56. Luke 1:32–35, 43.

57. Luke 2:21.

58. JST, Matthew 1:25.

59. Leviticus 12:2–3; see Baruch A. Levine, *The JPS Torah Commentary: Leviticus* (Philadelphia: The Jewish Publication Society, 1989), pp. 72–75.

60. Luke 2:22–24; see also Leviticus 12:1–8.

61. Josephus, *Against Apion,* II.8; see William Whiston, trans., *Josephus: Complete Works* (Grand Rapids, Michigan: Kregel Publications, 1972), p. 627.

62. Josephus, *Jewish Wars,* V. 198; see William Whiston, trans., *Josephus: Complete Works,* p. 554.

63. See Exodus 38:8.

64. See Benjamin Mazar, "Excavations Near Temple Mount Reveal Splendors of Herodian Jerusalem," *Biblical Archaeology Review* 6 (July/August 1980):44–59.

65. See Peretz Segal, "The Penalty of the Warning Inscription from the Temple of Jerusalem," *Israel Exploration Journal* 39 (1989):79–84.

66. See Mark 12:41–44.

67. See John 8:2–11.

68. The archaeological work in Jerusalem since 1968 demonstrates that the descriptions of the temple were not exaggerated by first-century witnesses; see Jack Finegan, *The Archeology of the New Testament: The Life of Jesus and the Beginning of the Early Church* (Princeton, New Jersey: Princeton University Press, 1992, rev. ed.), pp. 194–97.

69. Luke 2:36.
70. Luke 2:37.
71. See Luke 4:17–19.
72. Luke 1:38.
73. Luke 2:34–35.
74. Matthew 2:1, 9–11; italics added.
75. See Matthew 2:16.
76. Matthew 2:13.
77. Matthew 2:16.
78. Matthew 2:18; see also Jeremiah 31:5.
79. See Peter Garnsey, "Child Rearing in Ancient Italy," in David I. Kertzer and Richard P. Saller, eds., *The Family in Italy from Antiquity to the Present* (New Haven: Yale University Press, 1991), pp. 48–65.
80. See Luke 2:42.
81. See Luke 2:42–51; see also Deuteronomy 16:16.
82. Although an ordinary day's journey varied from eighteen to thirty miles, the first day's journey was customarily much shorter, usually three to eight miles from the starting place. Thus, if something were left behind, someone could return for it and easily catch up with the traveling caravan the next day. This might have been the case with Joseph and Mary, who would have immediately noticed their son's absence had they been traveling alone rather than with a large group. See James M. Freeman, *Manners and Customs of the Bible* (Plainfield, New Jersey: Logos International, rep. 1972), p. 409.
83. See Luke 2:41–46.
84. Luke 2:48–51.
85. See Max Zerwick and Mary Grosvenor, *A Grammatical Analysis of the Greek New Testament* (Rome: Biblical Institute Press, 1981), p. 181.
86. See Luke 2:52.

Chapter 7. Once More Astonished

1. For an example of this last category, see Matthew 18:23–25; Luke 12:51–53.
2. For example, see Mark 2:21; Matthew 13:33; Mark 2:22; Luke 5:31; Luke 22:27; Luke 15:8; Matthew 11:16–17.

3. This may also be why Jesus chose two examples, one male and one female, in his famous Matthew 24 sermon about the coming of the Son of Man: "Then shall two be in the field; the one shall be taken, the other left. Two women shall be grinding at the mill; the one shall be taken and the other left." (Matthew 24:40–41).

4. See Luke 18:1–8; 18:9–14.

5. Luke 18:2.

6. The word is less influenced by the Septuagint and more by ordinary Hellenistic usage; see Gottlob Schrenk, *"Ekdikeo," Theological Dictionary of the New Testament,* ed. Gerhard Kittel, 10 vols. (Grand Rapids, Michigan: Wm. B. Eerdmans Publishing Company, 1982), 2:446.

7. Luke 18:5.

8. Luke 18:6.

9. Luke 18:7–8.

10. Luke 13:18–21; Matthew 13:31–33; Matthew 13:44–46.

11. Luke 15:1, 4, 8.

12. Luke 15:9.

13. The Greek word used here for neighbours (*getonas*) could be used for either masculine or feminine neighbors, but the context may indicate female neighbors; the Greek word used here for friends (*philas*) means "women friends"; see William F. Arndt and F. Wilbur Gingrich, eds., *A Greek-English Lexicon of the New Testament and Other Early Christian Literature* (Chicago: University of Chicago Press, 1957), pp. 152, 868–69.

14. Luke 15:10; italics added.

15. See Matthew 13 and Luke 13.

16. Matthew 13:33.

17. Normal Jewish usage during the first century avoided the name of God, for which heaven was substituted. As a Gospel especially written for the Jews, Matthew maintains this practice.

18. Flavius Josephus, *Antiquities,* XVI.1; see William Whiston, trans., *Josephus: Complete Works* (Grand Rapids, Michigan: Kregel Publications, 1972), p. 336.

19. Flavius Josephus, *Antiquities,* XIV.330; see William Whiston, trans., *Josephus: Complete Works,* p. 306.

20. Matthew 18:23–27; italics added.

21. See Matthew 18:28–34.

22. In Roman law, a creditor could keep those in debt bondage

in chains; and ultimately, according to the most probable interpretation of the *Law of the Twelve Tables,* they might cut up the individual in pieces and divide the parts among themselves; see G. E. M. de ste. Croix, *The Class Struggle in the Ancient Greek World* (Ithaca, New York: Cornell University Press, 1981), pp. 162–74.

23. Luke 4:16–21; see also Isaiah 61:1–2.

24. John 16:21.

25. John 16:22.

26. The most complete edition of these materials is found in James H. Charlesworth, ed., *The Old Testament Pseudepigrapha,* 2 vols. (Garden City, New York: Doubleday & Company, Inc., 1983–1985).

27. See "Parousia," Bible Dictionary, LDS Edition of the King James Version of the Bible, p. 742.

28. Matthew 25:1–13, 14–30, 31–36.

29. Matthew 26.

30. Matthew 25:1–13.

31. See Matthew 24:45–51.

32. Matthew 24:37, 40–42.

33. Luke 7:36–50.

34. Luke 7:37–38.

35. *Shema,* the first Hebrew word translated "hear" in the following prayer: "Hear, O Israel, the Lord our God, the Lord is one, and you shall love the Lord your God with all your heart, and with all your soul, and with all your might" (Deuteronomy 6:4–5).

36. *Mishnah,* Ketuboth 7.6; see Herbert Danby, trans., *The Mishnah: Translated from the Hebrew with Introduction and Brief Explanatory Notes* (New York: Oxford University Press, 1974), p. 255.

37. Luke 7:38.

38. Luke 7:39.

39. Luke 7:40–43.

40. Luke 7:44–50.

Chapter 8. Wives, Mothers, and Daughters

1. Even among the Pharisees, two competing schools (known as Houses) debated the interpretation of Mosaic regulations based

on the teachings of Hillel and Shammai—first-century pharisaic leaders; see Anthony J. Saldarini, "Pharisees," *The Anchor Bible Dictionary,* ed. David Noel Freeman, 6 vols. (New York: Doubleday, 1992), 5:289–303.

2. See, for example, Matthew 15:3; Mark 7:8.

3. Matthew 5:27–30.

4. JST, Matthew 5:28; italics added.

5. See Exodus 20:14, 17.

6. Matthew 5:31–32.

7. See Deuteronomy 24:1–4.

8. On the other hand, another Pharisee, Shammai, argued that divorce was justified only as a result of adultery; see Robert W. Wall, "Divorce," *The Anchor Bible Dictionary,* 2:218.

9. *Mishnah,* Gittin 9.10; see Herbert Danby, trans., *The Mishnah: Translated from the Hebrew with Introduction and Brief Explanatory Notes* (New York: Oxford University Press, 1974), p. 321.

10. See Proverbs 5:15f; Malachi 2:14–16; *Babylonian Talmud,* Gittin 90b, *Tractate Gittin,* 90b, volume 14 in I. Epstein, ed., *Hebrew-English Edition of the Babylonian Talmud,* 25 vols. (London: Soncino Press, 1989); see also S. G. Wilson, *Luke and Law* (Cambridge: Cambridge University Press, 1983), p. 30.

11. See E. P. Sanders, *Judaism: Practice and Belief, 63 BCE–CE* (Philadelphia: Trinity Press International, 1992), p. 347.

12. See Matthew 19:3–12; Mark 10:2–12.

13. Mark 10:2–9.

14. Mark 10:10–12.

15. Mark 7:9–13.

16. See "Corban," Bible Dictionary, LDS Edition of the King James Version of the Bible, p. 650.

17. Mark 7:10.

18. See Max Zerwick and Mary Grosvenor, *Grammatical Analysis of the Greek New Testament* (Rome: Biblical Institute Press, 1981), p. 127.

19. *Papyri Oxyrhynchus,* IV.742; see Bernard P. Grenfell and Arthur S. Hunt, eds., *The Oxyrhynchus Papyri,* Part IV (London: Egypt Exploration Society, 1973, reprint), pp. 243–44.

20. See Keith R. Bradley, *Discovering the Roman Family: Studies in Roman Social History* (New York: Oxford University Press, 1990), especially the section, "Child Labor in the Roman World," pp. 112–19.

21. See Mark 9:33–37; 10:13–16.

22. Mark 9:33–37.

23. The term is used for a *"very young child, infant,* used of boys and girls," William F. Arndt and F. Wilbur Gingrich, *A Greek-English Lexicon of the New Testament and Other Early Christian Literature* (Chicago: University of Chicago Press, 1957), p. 608.

24. The greek word means: *"take, receive. . . . receive* as a guest, *welcome"*; see William F. Arndt and F. Wilbur Gingrich, *Greek–English Lexicon of the New Testament,* p. 176.

25. Mark 10:13.

26. See Luke 18:15.

27. Luke 18:16.

28. See Mark 10:17–27.

29. Luke 17:32.

30. Luke 4:25–26; see also 1 Kings 17.

31. Matthew 12:42.

32. See 1 Kings 10:1; 2 Chronicles 9:1.

33. Matthew 18:20.

34. *Pesahim* 64a; see *Tractate Pesahim* 65a, volume 5 in I. Epstein, ed., *Hebrew-English Edition of the Babylonian Talmud,* 25 vols. (London: Soncino Press, 1989).

35. *Midrash Rabbah* (Numbers) XI.5; see H. Freedman and Maurice Simon, eds., *Midrash Rabbah,* 10 vols. (London: Soncino Press, 1951), 5:433.

36. Luke 11:27.

37. Luke 11:28.

38. See Luke 1:45.

39. Deuteronomy 25:5–10; see also "Levirate Marriage," Bible Dictionary, LDS Edition of the King James Version of the Bible, p. 724.

40. Matthew 22:23–28.

41. See Mark 13:30, 7.

42. Mark 13:1–2.

43. Mark 13:17.

Chapter 9. Along the Way

1. Acts 10:38.

2. See Isaiah 61:1–2.

3. See Mark 1:21.

4. Estimates range from one quarter to one and a half million inhabitants. We may never know the true numbers, since ancient records notoriously inflated statistics. We have therefore taken a middle position on numbers and statistics throughout this work.

5. Mark 1:22.

6. Mark 1:27.

7. See Matthew 10:7–8.

8. Luke 7:11.

9. Luke 7:1.

10. Luke 7:12–15.

11. See the previous episode in Luke 7:2–10.

12. Luke 7:12.

13. *Midrash Rabbah,* Genesis, LXXI.6; see H. Freedman and Maurice Simon, eds., *Midrash Rabbah,* 10 vols. (London: Soncino Press, 1951), 1:657.

14. John 8:2–4.

15. See Numbers 5:11–31; see also Jacob Milgrom, *The JPS Torah Commentary: Numbers* (Philadelphia: Jewish Publication Society, 1990), pp. 37–43.

16. See Numbers 5:17.

17. Numbers 5:21.

18. *Babylonian Talmud,* Sotah 7a; see *Tractate Sotah* 7a, volume 13, I. Epstein, ed., *Hebrew-English Edition of the Babylonian Talmud,* 25 vols. (London: Soncino Press, 1989).

19. See Numbers 5:18.

20. See Ezekiel 16:39; Hosea 2:5.

21. Deuteronomy 19:15; however, there is some evidence that one witness was sufficient.

22. John 8:5–6.

23. See Leviticus 20:10.

24. See Mark 12:13–17 for a similar dilemma.

25. John 8:6; italics added.

26. John 8:7.

27. See Deuteronomy 17:7.

28. John 8:7.

29. See Bruce M. Metzger, *A Textual Commentary on the Greek New Testament* (New York: United Bible Societies, 1975), p. 222.

30. John 8:8.

31. John 8:10–11.

32. JST, John 8:11.
33. Matthew 21:23, 32.
34. Mark 3:8.
35. Exodus 20:8–11; Deuteronomy 5:12–15.
36. Numbers 15:32–36.
37. Leviticus 4:27–31.
38. According to Mark and Luke, the first miracle of healing takes place in a synagogue, as also the only Sabbath healing in Mark and Matthew; see Wolfgang Schrage, *"Synagoge," Theological Dictionary of the New Testament,* ed. Gerhard Kittel, 10 vols. (Grand Rapids, Michigan: Wm. B. Eerdmans Publishing Company, 1971), 7:830–33.
39. Luke 13:10–13.
40. Luke 21:28; italics added.
41. William F. Arndt and F. Wilbur Gingrich, *A Greek-English Lexicon of the New Testament and Other Early Christian Literature* (Chicago: University of Chicago Press, 1957), p. 56; see also Hebrews 12:12.
42. Luke 13:14.
43. Luke 13:16.
44. Mark 12:41–42.
45. Mark 12:43–44.
46. See, for example Exodus 22:2; Deuteronomy 10:18; Isaiah 1:17; Zechariach 7:10.
47. Mark 12:40.
48. See William F. Arndt and F. Wilbur Gingrich, *A Greek-English Lexicon of the New Testament,* pp. 656, 857.
49. Mark 5:35–43.
50. See Leviticus 15:19–33; other circumstances that rendered an individual unclean were leprosy and other skin diseases, contact with a corpse, and bodily emissions of all types.
51. See Numbers 19:12–16.
52. Mark 5:22–24.
53. Mark 5:35–38.
54. Matthew 9:23.
55. Mark 5:39–40.
56. Mark 5:40–43; italics added. Since *Thaleththi* (Talitha) has been attested in an epitaph dating from the first century A.D., this Aramaic phrase might better be translated, "Talitha, stand up!"; see Max Wilcox, "Talitha Cumi," *The Anchor Bible Dictionary,* ed.

David Noel Freedman, 6 vols. (New York: Doubleday, 1992), 6:310.

57. Mark 5:25–27. Others did the same; see, for example, Mark 6:56.

58. Luke 8:43.

59. Mark 5:27–28.

60. See Numbers 15:38–40; Deuteronomy 22:12.

61. See Judith Plaskow, *Standing Again at Sinai* (San Francisco: Harper Collins, 1990), p. 177.

62. Luke 8:44.

63. Mark 5:30.

64. Mark 5:31.

65. See Matthew 9:20–22; Luke 8:45.

66. Mark 5:32.

67. Mark 5:33.

68. Mark 5:34.

69. 1 Samuel 1:17.

70. See Francis Brown, S.R. Driver, and Charles A. Briggs, eds., *A Hebrew and English Lexicon of the Old Testament* (Oxford: The Clarendon Press, 1972), p. 1022.

Chapter 10. They Sat at Jesus' Feet

1. See Luke 10:38–42; John 11:1–12:11. Some have suggested that Simon the leper was her father and Judas was her brother.

2. Since the Middle Ages (and to the present), Mary has been confused with the "sinner" who anointed Jesus feet in Luke 7, who has been quite wrongly identified with Mary Magdalene. Graphic artists, poets, and Christian theologians have fallen victim to this fusing of persons; see Jane Schaber, "How Mary Magdalene Became a Whore," *Bible Review* (October 1992):30–37.

3. Luke 10:39.

4. A parallel is found in Acts when Paul defended himself to a Jewish crowd: "I am verily a man which am a Jew, born in Tarsus, a city in Cilicia, yet brought up in this city at *the feet of Gamaliel,* and taught according to the perfect manner of the law of the fathers, and was zealous toward God, as ye all are this day" (Acts 22:3; italics added).

5. See Luke 10:42.

6. Luke 10:38–39.

7. *Palestinian Talmud,* Sotah 19a; as cited in Abraham Cohen, *Everyman's Talmud* (New York: Schocken Books, 1975), p. 179.

8. *Babylonian Talmud,* Sotah 21a; see *Tractate Sotah* 21a, volume 13 in I. Epstein, ed., *Hebrew-English Edition of the Babylonian Talmud,* 25 vols. (London: Soncino Press, 1989).

9. *Babylonian Talmud,* Berakoth 17a, see *Tractate Berakoth* 17a, volume 1 in I. Epstein, ed., *Hebrew-English Edition of the Babylonian Talmud.*

10. Deuteronomy 31:12; italics added. Jesus makes the same point in Luke 11:27–28.

11. *Mishnah,* Aboth 1:4; see Herbert Danby, trans., *The Mishnah: Translated from the Hebrew with Introduction and Brief Explanatory Notes* (New York: Oxford University Press, 1974), p. 446.

12. See Luke 6:47.

13. See Luke 8:21; John 12:1–8.

14. Luke 14:25–27.

15. Matthew 10:34–39.

16. Luke 14:26; italics added.

17. JST, Luke 14:26; italics added.

18. See William F. Arndt and F. Wilbur Gingrich, *A Greek-English Lexicon of the New Testament and Other Early Christian Literature* (Chicago: University of Chicago Press, 1957), pp. 486–87.

19. As in the New Testament Church, the scriptures were not interpreted by the trained scribes, who knew all the nuances and parallels, but simply by reading them and quoting them in the light of what had happened in the life, atonement, and resurrection of the risen Christ.

20. See Mark 10:35; Luke 8:3; John 12:2.

21. See Mark 1:13.

22. See Mark 10:45; Luke 22:27; 12:37; see also John 13:1–11.

23. See William F. Arndt and F. Wilbur Gingrich, *A Greek-English Lexicon of the New Testament,* p. 30.

24. Mark 1:15.

25. See William F. Arndt and F. Wilbur Gingrich, *A Greek-English Lexicon of the New Testament,* p. 513.

26. Mark 8:34–36.

27. Luke 9:23; Matthew 19:28 ff.

28. Mark 1:17.

29. Matthew 22:1–14; Luke 14:16–24.

30. See also Matthew 8:14–15.

31. Mark 1:21; this synagogue has been found, see James F. Strange and Hershel Shanks, "Synagogue Where Jesus Preached Found at Capernaum," *Biblical Archaeology Review* 9 (November/December 1983):24–31.

32. Mark 1:22.

33. Mark 1:28.

34. Mark 1:29–31; italics added. Mark records, with a slight variation, Peter's own recollection of the events because his Gospel was probably written under Peter's direction. The awkwardness of the phrase, "And they entered into the house of Simon and Andrew, *with James and John*," is clarified with the direct speech of Peter, "We came into our house *with James and John*."

35. See James F. Strange and Hershel Shanks, "Has the House Where Jesus Stayed in Capernaum Been Found?" *Biblical Archaeology Review* 8 (November/December 1982):26–37.

36. See Helmut Koester, *"Synecho" Theological Dictionary of the New Testament,* ed. Gerhard Kittel, 10 vols. (Grand Rapids, Michigan, 1984), 7:877–79, 883; here the basic meaning of *synecho* is given as "to enclose," "lick up," . . . "to take or hold captive," and developing out of these meanings, "to oppress," "overpower," "rule."

37. See Luke 4:35.

38. See Luke 4:16–19, where Jesus reads from Isaiah 61:1–2.

39. See Mark 1:13.

40. See for example, Revised Standard Version (RSV), Mark 1:13, 31; *The New Oxford Annotated Bible with the Apocrypha: Revised Standard Version* (New York: Oxford University Press, 1977).

41. Matthew 26–28.

42. Mark 1:31–34.

43. It is interesting to note that Peter's wife went with him on some of his missionary journeys; see 1 Corinthians 9:5.

44. See John 4:3–30, 39–42.

45. John 2:13–25; 3:1–21.

46. John 4:9.

47. John 4:20.

48. John 3:1–21.

49. John 4:9.

50. See John 4:9.

51. A First-Century Rabbinical dictum cited in Raymond E. Brown, *The Gospel According to John*, 2 vols. (Garden City, New York: Doubleday & Company, Inc., 1966), 1:170.

52. See John 8:48 for such an example: "Say we not well that thou art a Samaritan, and hast a devil?"

53. See John 1:6–13.

54. See John 3:12–17; later, Nicodemus did reappear as he defended Jesus to the Pharisees (see John 7:50) and brought spices to his burial (see John 19:39).

55. John 4:29–30.

56. See John 4:28.

57. John 4:39–42; italics added.

58. See Deuteronomy 18:18; the Samaritans only accepted the five books of Moses, not the rest of the Jewish scriptures.

59. See Mark 7:24–30.

60. Mark 7:24.

61. Mark 7:27.

62. Mark 7:28.

63. Mark 7:29.

64. See Matthew 15:21–28.

65. Matthew 15:28.

66. See Matthew 15:22.

67. Luke 10:38.

68. Luke 10:40.

69. Luke 10:40.

70. Luke 10:41–42.

71. See Luke 10:40–42.

72. Mark 5:43.

73. See Luke 12:22–23, 30–31.

74. Genesis 46:1.

75. The Jerusalem Bible, 1 Samuel 3:4 (the KJV translators missed the double naming found in the Hebrew); *Jerusalem Bible: Reader's Edition* (Garden City, New York: Doubleday & Company, Inc., 1968), p. 298.

76. Acts 9:4.

77. Mark 1:16–20.

78. See, for example, the calling of the rich young ruler in Luke 18:18–23.

79. See Luke 8:1–3.

80. John 11:38–44.

81. John 11:5.

82. John 11:3.

83. John 11:18.

84. See L. Y. Rahmani, "Ancient Jerusalem's Funerary Customs and Tombs—Part One," *Biblical Archeologist* 44 (Summer 1981):171–77.

85. John 11:19.

86. John 11:20.

87. John 11:21–22.

88. John 15:7.

89. John 11:25–26.

90. John 11:27.

91. See Matthew 16:16.

92. See John 11:33–35.

93. John 11:41–44.

94. See Matthew 21:8; Mark 11:8; Luke 19:36.

95. John 12:12–15; see also Zechariah 9:9.

96. Luke 23:27–33; see also Hosea 10:8.

97. See Luke 23:33.

98. John 2:1–11. The site of New Testament Cana is unknown, but in all likelihood it is situated some eight miles north of Nazareth across the Bet Netofa Valley; see map 15, "Jesus' Galilean Ministry," and "Cana of Galilee," Bible Dictionary, LDS Edition of the King James Version of the Bible, p. 629.

99. See John 2:1–11; 1:35–51.

100. John 2:1.

101. John 2:2.

102. Mary seems to have had some responsibilities at the wedding feast; therefore, it could have easily been a wedding of a relative of Jesus, possibly one of his younger half-brothers or half-sisters.

103. See John 2:3–4.

104. The Joseph Smith Translation states: "Jesus said unto her, Woman, what wilt thou have me do for thee? that I will do; for mine hour is not yet come" (JST, John 2:4).

105. John 2:6.

106. John 2:6.

107. John 2:7–9.

108. The wedding imagery is picked up in the story of John the Baptist (John 3:25–30), where John describes in the language of a bride and bridegroom his joy at the coming of Jesus.

109. Mark 6:3; see also Matthew 13:56; Mark 3:32.

110. Matthew 13:55–56.

111. 1:24–25.

112. John 7:3, 5.

113. Mark 3:21.

114. Mark 6, 14.

115. New International Version (NIV), Mark 3:21; italics added; in *The NIV Study Bible: New International Version* (Grand Rapids, Michigan: Zondervan Bible Publishers, 1985), p. 1498.

116. Mark 6:4.

117. John 16:32.

118. John 19:25–27.

119. Acts 1:13–14.

Chapter 11. Certain Women Which Had Been Healed

1. See Luke 8:1–3; the King James Version (KJV) rightly preserves the traditional reading of several ancient manuscript authorities that have the women ministering to "him" (that is, to Jesus alone), instead of "them," which some other versions use; see, for example, NIV, Luke 8:3, The NIV Study Bible: New International Version, ed. Kenneth Barker (Grand Rapids, Michigan: Zondervan Bible Publishers, 1985), p. 1553. This is confirmed by Mark 15:41 and Matthew 27:55, where the women who had followed Jesus from Galilee, minister to *him*. This later reading of Luke tends to subordinate the role of women.

2. See, for example, Matthew 5:44. Jesus seemed to be referring to the Essenes' writings, "to love all the children of light . . . and to hate all the children of darkness" 1QS 1.4; see "The Manual of Discipline," in Theodor H. Gaster, ed., *The Dead Sea Scriptures* (New York: Doubleday, 1976), p. 44.

3. Even today in popular tradition, Mary Magdalene represents the repentant sinner, lifted from the depths of sin (prostitution), proof that even the lowliest can be saved through repen-

tance and devotion to Jesus. Yet this is a very different picture from the one the Gospels give us; see Jane Schaber, "How Mary Magdalene Became a Whore," *Bible Review* 8 (October 1992):30–37.

4. Matthew 15:39.

5. See Luke 8:2; Mark 16:9.

6. See Luke 8:2–3.

7. Antipas was appointed tetrarch of Galilee and Perea, which he ruled from 4 B.C. to A.D. 39. He continued his father's building program; first enlarged his capital, Sepphoris; then built a second on the shores of the Sea of Galilee, which he called "Tiberias" in honor of the emperor. Jesus called him the "fox" (Luke 13:32). He also appears in Luke 23:6 as Jesus' sovereign, to whom Jesus is sent by Pilate for interrogation; see "Herod," Bible Dictionary, LDS Edition of the King James Version of the Bible, p. 701.

8. See William F. Arndt and F. Wilbur Gingrich, *A Greek-Lexicon of the New Testament and Other Early Christian Literature* (Chicago: University of Chicago Press, 1957), p. 303.

9. See Luke 8:2–3.

10. Matthew 27:56.

11. Mark 15:40.

12. Luke 23:49.

13. Luke 24:10.

14. John 19:25.

15. See Mark 1:16–20; Luke 5:1–11.

16. Mark 1:20.

17. Mark 15:41.

18. Luke 22:24; see also Matthew 20:20–27; Mark 10:35–44. While some harmonies do not place the Luke account with Matthew and Mark, we believe the context of the story does allow such a parallel.

19. Matthew 20:20–21.

20. Matthew 20:24.

21. NIV, Psalm 127:3–4; The NIV Study Bible: New International Version, p. 925.

22. Luke 22:25–27.

23. For a complete discussion of Greco-Roman background of this term, see Paul Veyne, *Bread and Circuses: Historical Sociology and Political Pluralism* (New York: Allen Lane The Penguin Press, 1990).

24. Charlton T. Lewis, *An Elementary Latin Dictionary* (Oxford: Clarendon Press, 1977), p. 588.

25. Luke 23:49; italics added.

Chapter 12. A Memorial of Her

1. See Isaiah 53; Mark 8:29–33.

2. See Richard Neitzel Holzapfel, "The Hidden Messiah," *A Witness of Jesus Christ: The 1989 Sperry Symposium on the Old Testament,* ed. by Richard D. Draper (Salt Lake City: Deseret Book Co., 1990), pp. 80–95.

3. See Mark 8:32.

4. Mark 10:32.

5. Matthew 26:1–4; italics added.

6. "And it came to pass, when Jesus had ended these sayings," Matthew 7:28. "And it came to pass, when Jesus had made an end of commanding his twelve disciples," Matthew 11:1. "And it came to pass, that when Jesus had finished these parables," Matthew 13:53. "And it came to pass, that when Jesus had finished these sayings," Matthew 19:1.

7. Matthew 26:6.

8. See Matthew 28:1–2; see also Mark 16:1; Luke 23:55–24:3; John 20:1.

9. The Synoptic tradition speaks of the house of Simon the leper—some have suggested that Simon was the father of Lazarus, Mary, and Martha, thus eliminating the seemingly contradiction on the location of the event; see endnote 16, below.

10. John 11:18.

11. John 12:1–2.

12. See William F. Arndt and F. Wilbur Gingrich, *A Greek-English Lexicon of the New Testament and Other Early Christian Literature* (Chicago: University of Chicago Press, 1957), p. 55.

13. John 12:13; see also Luke 10:39; John 11:32.

14. John 12:3.

15. Mark 14:5.

16. John 12:4–5; see Matthew 26:8 and Mark 14:4 for the inclusion of the other disciples in this protest). Judas is here identified as the son of Simon, which may make him the brother of Martha, Mary, and Lazarus; see endnote 9 above.

17. Mark 14:4–5; italics added.

18. See Max Zerwick and Mary Grosvenor, *A Grammatical Analysis of the Greek New Testament* (Rome: Biblical Institute Press, 1981), p. 154; and William F. Arndt and F. Wilbur Gingrich, *A Greek-English Lexicon of the New Testament*, p. 254.

19. John 12:7–8.

20. JST, John 12:7, italics added; see also JST, Matthew 26:12–13; JST, Mark 14:8.

21. See for example, the discussion of Mark's verse in Max Zerwick and Mary Grosvenor, *A Grammatical Analysis of the Greek New Testament*, p. 154.

22. John 12:1–20; see also LDS D&C 88:138–41.

23. John 13:34–35.

24. Mark 14:9; see also Matthew 26:13.

25. JST, Mark 14:8–9; italics added.

26. John 12:3.

27. *Midrash Rabbah,* Ecclesiastes, VII:i; see H. Freeman and Maurice Simon, eds., *Midrash Rabbah,* 10 vols. (London: Soncino Press, 1951), 7:167.

28. John 11:2.

29. See John 12:3; Mark 14:3; Matthew 26:7.

30. See William F. Arndt and F. Wilbur Gingrich, *A Greek-English Lexicon of the New Testament*, p. 895.

31. See Matthew 26:69–72; see also Mark 14:66–72; Luke 22:56–62.

32. Matthew 27:19; italics added.

33. See Matthew 27:55–61; see also Mark 15:40–47; Luke 23:49–56; John 19:25–27.

Chapter 13. The Last to Remain, the First to Return and Remember

1. See Joseph Plevnik, "The Eyewitnesses of the Risen Jesus in Luke 24," *The Catholic Biblical Quarterly* 49 (January 1987):90–103.

2. Luke 23:53.

3. Luke 23:53.

4. Luke 23:55–56.

5. Luke 24:1.

6. See Luke 23:49, 54.

7. Luke 24:1.

8. See Luke 24:5–7, 10–11.

9. Some have seen Luke's phrase "two men," an added description of the angels, as a device that underscores that the two were legitimate witnesses; see also 9:30; Acts 1:10.

10. Josephus, *Antiquities* IV.219; see William Whiston, trans., *Josephus: Complete Works* (Grand Rapids, Michigan: Kregel Publications, 1972), p. 97.

11. See Luke 24:12.

12. Luke 24:5–8.

13. See Luke 24:8.

14. See Luke 24:6, 8.

15. Luke 9:22–23.

16. See Luke 8:1–3.

17. See Luke 9:23.

18. Luke 24:9.

19. Luke 24:10.

20. See Luke 23:49.

21. See Luke 9:45; 18:34.

22. Luke 24:13–35.

23. Luke 24:13, 15; the furlong, a Greek measurement still used in Roman times, was about six hundred feet, the length of the racetrack at Olympia. This clue helps us identify the location of the village from several possible sites. In all likelihood, Emmaus Colonia, situated one to two hours' walking distance from Jerusalem is the probable location; for another possible identification see "Emmaus," Bible Dictionary, LDS Edition of the King James Version of the Bible, p. 665.

24. "And the one of them, whose name was Cleopas" (Luke 24:18) is not to be confused, as often is the case, with Cleophas of John 19:25, whose name is of Semetic origin, whereas Cleopas is well attested as a Greek name (a shortened form of Kleopatros— "illustrious father"); see Robert F. O'Toole, "Cleopas," *Anchor Bible Dictionary,* ed. David Noel Freedman, 6 vols. (New York: Doubleday, 1992), 1:1063–64.

25. See Luke 24:29–30.

26. Luke 24:17–24.

27. Luke 24:16.

28. See Luke 24:19–21, 23.

29. See Luke 24:26.
30. Luke 24:25–26.
31. Luke 24:27–31.
32. Luke 24:31.
33. Luke 24:32.
34. Luke 24:33–35.
35. Luke 24:34.
36. Luke 22:15–29.
37. See Acts 12:12.
38. Luke 24:36–40.
39. Luke 24:33.
40. See Luke 24:33, 38–40.
41. Matthew 27:51; italics added.
42. Matthew 28:2; italics added.
43. See Matthew 28:9–10.
44. Matthew 28:8–10.
45. Mark 16:1.
46. Mark 16:14.
47. See John 20:1–10, 11–18.
48. John 20:2.
49. John 20:11.
50. John 20:13.
51. John 20:13.
52. See John 20:2; italics added.
53. John 20:15.
54. John 1:38.
55. John 20:15.
56. See Numbers 19:11, 16, 19; 31:19, 24; see also Jacob Milgrom, *The JPS Torah Commentary Numbers* (Philadelphia: New York, 1990), pp. 160–63, 260–61.
57. John 20:16–17.
58. John 10:3.
59. John 10:4.
60. See John 11:43.
61. See John 20:18.
62. JST, John 20:17.
63. John 20:17.
64. Greek text of John 20:18.
65. Psalm 22:22; italics added.
66. See Gottfried Quell, *"Kurios," Theological Dictionary of the*

New Testament, ed. Gerhard Kittel, 10 vols. (Grand Rapids, Michigan: Wm. B. Eerdmans Publishing Company, 1982), 3:1058–81; in particular 1060–62.

67. See "Apostle," Bible Dictionary, LDS Edition of the King James Version of the Bible, p. 612.

Chapter 14. Neither Male nor Female

1. See Adolf von Harnack, *The Mission and Expansion of Christianity During the First Three Centuries* (London: Williams and Norgate, 1908), pp. 64–84.

2. Averil Cameron, "'Neither Male nor Female,'" *Greece and Rome* 27 (April 1980):60–68.

3. Origen, *Contra Celsus,* 3.49; see A. Cleveland Coxe, ed., "Origen against Celsus," *The Ante-Nicene Fathers,* 10 vols. (Grand Rapids, Michigan: Wm. B. Eerdmans Publishing Company, 1989), 4:484.

4. Matthew 9:36–37.

5. Matthew 9:38.

6. See Luke 10:2.

7. Acts 1:14.

8. See Acts 9:2; 19:23; 22:4; 24:22.

9. *Babylonian Talmud,* Menahoth 43b; see *Tractate Menahoth* 43b, volume 23 in I. Epstein, ed., *Hebrew-English Edition of the Babylonian Talmud,* 25 volumes (London: Soncino Press, 1989).

10. Galatians 3:26–29.

---

1. Editions and Translations Cited or Quoted

Ancient Bible Editions

The Aramaic Bible: Targum Onqelos to Leviticus and Numbers. Wilmington, Delaware: Michael Glazier, Inc., 1988.

The Greek New Testament. ed. Kurt Aland, Matthew Black, Carlo M. Martini, Bruce M. Metzger, and Allen Wikgreen. New York: American Bible Society, 1975.

The Interlinear Greek-English New Testament. ed. Alfred Marshall. London: Samuel Bagster and Sons Limited, 1972.

The Septuagint with Apocrypha: Greek and English. trans. Sir Lancelot C. L. Branton. 1851. Reprint. Grand Rapids, Michigan: Zondervan Publishing House, 1975.

Modern Bible Editions

The Holy Bible. LDS Edition of the King James Version of the Bible. Salt Lake City: The Church of Jesus Christ of Latter-day Saints, 1978.

The Holy Scriptures: Inspired Version. Independence, Missouri: Herald Publishing House, 1974.

The Jerusalem Bible: Reader's Edition. Garden City, New York: Doubleday & Company, Inc., 1968.

The NIV Study Bible: New International Version. ed. Kenneth Barker. Grand Rapids, Michigan: Zondervan Bible Publishers, 1985.

The New Oxford Annotated Bible with the Apocrypha: Revised Standard Version. New York: Oxford University Press, 1977.

The Dead Sea Scrolls

The Dead Sea Scriptures. trans. Theodor H. Gaster. New York: Anchor Books, 1976.
The Temple Scroll. ed. Yigael Yadin. 3 vols. Jerusalem: The Israel Exploration Society, 1983.

Rabbinic Literature

Hebrew-English Edition of the Babylonian Talmud. ed. I. Epstein. 25 vols. London: Soncino Press, 1989.
The Mishnah: Translated from the Hebrew with Introduction and Brief Explanatory Notes. trans. Herbert Danby. Oxford: The Clarendon Press, 1974.
The Midrash Rabbah. ed. H. Freedman and Maurice Simon. 10 vols. New York: Soncino Press, 1951.
Abraham Cohen, ed. *Everyman's Talmud* (New York: Shocken Books, 1975).

Other Jewish Literature and Texts

Josephus. *Josephus: Complete Works.* trans. William Whiston. Grand Rapids, Michigan: Kregel Publications, 1972.
The Old Testament Pseudepigrapha. ed. James H. Charlesworth. 2 vols. Garden City, New York: Doubleday & Company, Inc., 1983–1985.

Other Ancient Literature

Aristotle. *On the Generation of Animals.* trans. A. L. Peck. Loeb Classical Library. Cambridge: Harvard University Press, 1953.
Cicero, *The Speeches.* trans. Lewis Lord. Loeb Classical Library Cambridge: Harvard University Press, 1959.
Demosthenes. *Private Orations.* trans. A. T. Murray. 3 vols. Loeb Classical Library. Cambridge: Harvard University Press, 1958.
Eusebius. *Ecclesiastical History.* Grand Rapids, Michigan: Baker Book House, 1991.

Hesiod. *Theogony, Works and Days, Shield.* trans. Apostolos N. Athanassakis. Baltimore: The Johns Hopkins University Press, 1983.

Origen. *The Ante-Nicene Fathers.* ed. Cleveland A. Coxe. Grand Rapids, Michigan: Wm. B. Erdmans Publishing Company, 1989.

The Oxyrhynchus Papyri. ed. Bernard P. Grenfell and Arthur S. Hunt. Part IV. London: Egypt Exploration Society, 1973.

Pliny. *Letters.* trans. William Melmoth. 2 vols. Loeb Classical Library. Cambridge: Harvard University Press, 1961.

Sophocles. *The Complete Greek Tragedies: Sophocles.* ed. David Grene and Richmond Lattimore. 2 vols. Chicago: The University of Chicago Press, 1959.

Tacitus. *The Histories.* trans. Clifford Moore. 2 vols. Loeb Classical Library. Cambridge: Harvard University Press, 1956.

2. Reference Works Cited or Quoted

The Anchor Bible Dictionary. ed. David Noel Freedman. 6 vols. New York: Doubleday, 1992.

An Elementary Latin Dictionary. ed. Charlton T. Lewis. Oxford: The Clarendon Press, 1977.

A Concise Etymological Dictionary of the English Language. ed. Walter W. Skeat. Oxford: Clarendon Press, 1976.

A Grammatical Analysis of the Greek New Testament. ed. Max Zerwick and Mary Grosvenor. Rome: Biblical Institute Press, 1981.

A Greek-English Lexicon of the New Testament and Other Early Christian Literature. ed. William F. Arndt and Wilbur F. Gingrich. Chicago: The University of Chicago Press, 1957.

A Hebrew and English Lexicon of the Old Testament. ed. Francis Brown, S.R. Driver and Charles A. Briggs. Oxford: The Clarendon Press, 1972.

Horizontal Harmony of the Four Gospels in Parallel Columns. ed. Thomas M. Mumford. Salt Lake City: Deseret Book Co., 1979.

An Intermediate Greek-English Lexicon. ed. Liddell and Scott. Oxford: Clarendon Press, 1975.

The Joseph Smith Translation of the Four Gospels: A Harmony. ed.

Steven J. Hite and Julie Melville Hite. Orem, Utah: S & J Publishing, 1989.

The Macmillan Bible Atlas ed. Yohanan Aharoni and Michael Avi-Yonah. New York: Macmillan Publishing Co., Inc., 1977. rev. ed.

The Oxford Classical Dictionary. ed. N. G. L. Hammond and H. H. Schullard. Oxford: Clarendon Press, 1976.

A Short Dictionary of the New Testament. ed. Albert Rouet. New York: Paulist Press, 1982.

A Textual Commentary on the Greek New Testament. ed. Bruce M. Metzger. New York: United Bible Societies, 1975.

Theological Dictionary of the New Testament. ed. Gerhard Kittel. 10 vols. Grand Rapids, Michigan: Wm. B. Eerdmans Publishing Company, 1982.

Synopse der drei ersten Evangelien/Synopsis of the First Three Gospels with the Addition of the Johannine Parallels. ed. Albert Huck. Tunbingen, W. Germany: J.C.B. Mohr [Paul Siebeck], 1981.

3. General

Albright, W. F. and C. S. Mann. *The Anchor Bible: Matthew*. Garden City, New York: Doubleday & Company, Inc., 1971.

Alfoldy, Geza. *The Social History of Rome*. Trans. David Braund and Frank Pollock. Baltimore: The Johns Hopkins University Press, 1988.

Anderson, Richard Lloyd. "The Testimony of Luke," in *Studies in Scripture: Volume Five, The Gospels*. ed. Kent P. Jackson and Robert L. Millet. Salt Lake City: Deseret Book Co., 1986. pp. 88–108.

Angel, J. Lawrence. "Ecology and Population in the Eastern Mediterranean," *World Archaeology* 4 (1972):88–105.

Armstrong, Karen. *The Gospel According to Woman: Christianity's Creation of the Sex War in the West*. New York: Anchor Books, 1987.

Baskin, Judith. "The Separation of Women in Rabbinic Judaism," in Ellison Findly and Yvonne Haddad, eds., *Women, Religion and Social Change*. Albany: State University of New York Press, 1984, 3–18.

Bell, James B. *The Roots of Jesus: A Genealogical Investigation.* Garden City, New York: Doubleday & Company, Inc., 1983.

Best, Ernest. *Disciples and Discipleship: Studies in the Gospel According to Mark.* Edinburgh: T. & T. Clark Ltd., 1986.

Brady, Keith R. *Discovering the Roman Family: Studies in Roman Social History.* New York: Oxford University Press, 1990.

Bridnenthal, R. and C. Koonz, eds. *Becoming Visible: Women in European History.* Boston: Houghton Mifflin, 1977.

Brooten, Bernadette J. *Women Leaders in the Ancient Synagogue.* Brown Judaic Studies 36. Chico: Scholars Press, 1982.

Brown, Raymond E. *The Anchor Bible: The Gospel According to John.* 2 vols. Garden City, New York: Doubleday & Company, Inc., 1970.

Brown, Raymond, Karl P. Donfried, Joseph A. Fitzmyer, and John Reumann. *Mary in the New Testament.* Philadelphia: Fortress Press, 1978.

Brown, Raymond E. *The Birth of the Messiah: A Commentary on the Infancy Narratives in Matthew and Luke.* Garden City, New York: Image Books, 1979.

Brown, S. Kent. "The Testimony of Mark," in *Studies in Scripture: Volume Five, The Gospels.* edited by Kent P. Jackson and Robert L. Millet. Salt Lake City: Deseret Book Co., 1986. pp. 61–87.

Buby, Bertrand. *Mary The Faithful Disciple.* New York: Paulist Press, 1985.

Cameron, Averil. "'Neither Male nor Female.'" *Greece & Rome* 27 (April 1980):60–68.

Cameron, Averil and Amelie Kuhrt. *Images of Women in Antiquity.* London: Croom Helm Ltd., 1983.

Camp, Claudia V. "Understanding a Patriarchy: Women in Second Century B.C. Jerusalem through the Eyes of Ben Sira." In Amy-Jill Levine, ed., *"Women Like This": New Perspectives on Jewish Women in the Greco-Roman World,* pp. 1–39. Atlanta: Scholars Press, 1991.

Cantarella, Eva. *Pandora's Daughters: The Role & Status of Women in Greek & Roman Antiquity.* Baltimore: The Johns Hopkins University Press, 1987.

Cantarella, Eva. *Bisexuality in the Ancient World.* New Haven: Yale University Press, 1992.

Charlesworth, James H. *Jesus and the Dead Sea Scrolls.* New York: Doubleday, 1992.

Cohen, Sheye J. D. *From the Maccabees to the Mishnah.* Philadelphia: Westminster Press, 1987.

Crossan, John Dominic. *The Historical Jesus: The Life of a Mediterranean Jewish Peasant.* San Francisco: HarpersSanFrancisco, 1991.

Cwiekoswki, Frederick J. *The Beginnings of the Church.* New York: Paulist Press, 1988.

Dandamayev, Muhammad A. "Slavery," *The Anchor Bible Dictionary.* Edited by David Noel Freedman. 6 vols. New York: Doubleday, 1992. 6:62.

Darr, Katheryn Pfisterer. *Far More Precious than Jewels: Perspectives on Biblical Women.* Louisville: Westminster/John Knox Press, 1991.

Daube, David. "Jesus and the Samaritan Woman: The Meaning of *synchraomai,*" *Journal of Biblical Literature* 69 (1950):137–47.

de Sainte. Croix, G.E.M. *The Class Struggle in the Ancient Greek World.* Ithaca: Cornell University Press, 1981.

Evans, Mary J. *Woman in the Bible.* Downers Grove, Illinois: InterVarsity Press, 1983.

Ferguson, Everett. *Backgrounds of Early Christianity.* Grand Rapids, Michigan: William B. Eerdmans Publishing Company, 1987.

Finegan, Jack. *The Archeology of the New Testament: The Life of Jesus and the Beginning of the Early Church.* Princeton, New Jersey: Princeton University Press, 1992, rev. ed.

Fiorenza, Elisabeth Schussler. *In Memory of Her: A Feminist Theological Reconstruction of Christian Origins.* New York: Crossroad, 1983.

Fitzmyer, Joseph A. *The Anchor Bible: The Gospel According to Luke.* 2 vols. Garden City, New York: Doubleday & Company, Inc., 1979.

Foley, Helene P., ed. *Reflections of Women in Antiquity.* New York: Gordon and Breach Science Publishers, 1981.

Freeman, James M. *Manners and Customs of the Bible.* Plainfield, New Jersey: Logos International, rep. 1972.

Freyen, Sean. *Galilee, Jesus and The Gospels: Literary Approaches and Historical Investigations.* Philadelphia: Fortress Press, 1988.

Gardner, Jane F. *Women in Roman Law & Society.* London: Croom Helm Ltd., 1986.

Garnsey, Peter. "Child Rearing in Ancient Italy," in David I. Kertzer and Richard P. Saller, eds., *The Family in Italy from Antiquity to the Present.* New Haven: Yale University Press, 1991. pp. 48–65.

Grant, Michael. *A Social History of Greece and Rome.* New York: Charles Scribner's Sons, 1992.

Grassi, Joseph A. *The Hidden Heroes of the Gospels: Female Counterparts of Jesus.* Collegeville, Minnesota: The Liturgical Press, 1989.

Griggs, C. Wilford. "The Testimony of John," in *Studies in Scripture: Volume Five, The Gospels.* ed. Kent P. Jackson and Robert L. Millet. Salt Lake City: Deseret Book Co., 1986. pp. 109–26.

Hallett, Judith P. "The Role of Women in Roman Elegy: Counter-Cultural Feminism," *Arethusa* 6 (1973):103–24.

Harnack, Adolf von. *The Mission and Expansion of Christianity During the First Three Centuries.* London: Williams and Norgate, 1908.

Hendrickx, Herman. *The Resurrection Narratives of the Synoptic Gospels.* London: Geoffrey Chapman, 1978.

Hoffman, R. Joseph. *Jesus Outside the Gospels.* Buffalo, New York: Prometheus Books, 1984.

Holzapfel, Richard Neitzel. "The Hidden Messiah," *A Witness of Jesus Christ: The 1989 Sperry Symposium on the Old Testament.* ed. Richard D. Draper. Salt Lake City: Deseret Book Co., 1990. pp. 80–95.

Holzapfel, Richard Neitzel. "The Passion of Jesus Christ," *The Lord of the Gospels: The 1990 Sperry Symposium on the New Testament.* ed. Bruce A. Van Orden and Brent L. Top. Salt Lake City: Deseret Book Co., 1991. pp. 69–82.

Itzchaky, S. M. Yitzhaki, and S. Kottek, "Fertility in Jewish Traditions," *Proceedings of the Second International Symposium on Medicine in the Bible and the Talmud, Koroth* 9 (1985):131.

Jeremias, Joachim. *Jerusalem in the Time of Jesus.* Philadelphia: Fortress Press, 1969.

Kinnear, Mary. *Daughters of Time: Women in the Western Tradition.* Ann Arbor: University of Michigan Press, 1982.

Koester, Helmut. *Introduction to the New Testament: History,*

Culture, and Religion of the Hellenistic Age. Philadelphia: Fortress Press, 1982.

Koester, Helmut. *Introduction to the New Testament: History and Literature of Early Christianity.* Philadelphia: Fortress Press, 1982.

Koester, Helmut. "*Synecho,*" *Theological Dictionary of the New Testament.* ed. Gerhard Kittel. 10 vols. Grand Rapids, Michigan: Wm. B. Eerdmans Publishing Company, 1982. 7:877–87.

Kraemer, Ross Shepard. *Her Share of the Blessings: Women's Religions among Pagans, Jews, and Christians in the Greco-Roman World.* New York: Oxford University Press, 1992.

Kummel, Werner Georg. *Introduction to the New Testament.* Nashville: Abingdon Press, 1975.

Lefkowitz, Mary R. and Maureen B. Fant, comp. *Women's Life in Greece & Rome: A Source Book in Translation.* Baltimore: Johns Hopkins University Press, 1992.

Levine, Amy-Jill, ed. *"Women Like This": New Perspectives on Jewish Women in the Greco-Roman World.* Atlanta: Scholars Press, 1991.

Levine, Baruch A., ed. *The JPS Torah Commentary: Leviticus.* Philadelphia: Jewish Publication Society, 1989.

Levine, L.I. "Herod the Great," *The Anchor Bible Dictionary* ed. David Noel Freedman. 6 vols. New York: Doubleday, 1992. 3:161–69.

Loades, Ann, ed. *Feminist Theology: A Reader.* London: SPCK, 1990.

MacHaffie, Barbara J., ed. *Readings in Her Story: Women in Christian Traditions.* Minneapolis: Fortress Press, 1992.

Maccoby, Hyam. *Judaism in the First Century.* London: Sheldon Press, 1989.

Macurdy, Grace. *Hellenistic Queens.* Baltimore: John Hopkins University Press, 1932.

McConkie, Bruce R. *Doctrinal New Testament Commentary: The Gospels.* Salt Lake City: Bookcraft, Inc., 1965.

McConkie, Bruce R. *The Mortal Messiah.* 4 vols. Salt Lake City: Deseret Book Co., 1979–1981.

Malina, Bruce J. and Richard L. Rohrbaugh. *Social-Science Commentary on the Synoptic Gospels.* Minneapolis: Fortress Press, 1992.

Mann, C. S. *The Anchor Bible: Mark.* Garden City, New York: Doubleday & Company, Inc., 1986.

Massey, Michael. *Women in Ancient Greece and Rome.* Cambridge: Cambridge University Press, 1988.

Matthews, Victor H. *Manners and Customs in the Bible: An Illustrated Guide to Daily Life in Bible Times.* Peabody, Massachusetts: Hendrickson Publishers, 1991, rev. ed.

Mazar, Benjamin. "Excavations Near Temple Mount Reveal Splendors of Herodian Jerusalem," *Biblical Archaeology Review* 6 (July/August 1980):44–59.

Meeks, Wayne A. "The Image of the Androgyne: Some Uses of a Symbol in Earliest Christianity," *History of Religions* 13 (February 1974):165–208.

Merkel, Helmut. "The Opposition between Jesus and Judaism," in *Jesus and the Politics of His Day.* ed. Ernst Bammel and C.F.D. Moule. Cambridge: Cambridge University Press, 1984. pp. 129–44.

Meyers, Carol. *Discovering Eve: Ancient Israelite Women in Context.* New York: Oxford University Press, 1988.

Milgrom, Jacob, ed. *The JPS Torah Commentary: Numbers.* Philadelphia: The Jewish Publication Society, 1990.

Millet, Robert L. "The Testimony of Matthew," in *Studies in Scripture: Volume Five, The Gospels.* ed. Kent P. Jackson and Robert L. Millet. Salt Lake City: Deseret Book Co., 1986. pp. 38–60.

Moltmann-Wendel, Elisabeth. *The Women around Jesus.* New York: Crossroad, 1992.

Moore, George Foote. *Judaism in the First Centuries of the Christian Era: The Age of the Tannaim.* 3 vols. Cambridge: Harvard University Press, 1927.

Neusner, Jacob. *Judaism in the Beginning of Christianity.* Philadelphia: Fortress Press, 1984.

Neusner, Jacob. "How Judaism & Christianity Can Talk To Each Other." *Bible Review* 6 (December 1990):32–45.

Neusner, Jacob. *Reading and Believing: Ancient Judaism and Contemporary Gullibility.* Atlanta: Scholars Press, 1986.

Neusner, Jacob. *A History of the Mishnaic Law of Women.* 5 vols. Leiden: E.J. Brill, 1980.

Newsom, Carol A. and Sharon H. Ringe, eds. *The Women's Bible*

Commentary. Louisville, Kentucky: Westminster/John Knox Press, 1992.

Nickelsburg, George W. E. and Michael E. Stone. *Faith and Piety in Early Judaism: Texts and Documents*. Philadelphia: Fortress Press, 1983.

O'Toole, Robert F. "Cleopas," *Anchor Bible Dictionary*. ed. David Noel Freedman, 6 vols. New York: Doubleday, 1992. pp. 1063–64.

Ogden, D. Kelly. *Where Jesus Walked: The Land and Culture of New Testament Times*. Salt Lake City: Deseret Book Company, 1991.

Pagels, Elaine. *Adam, Eve, and the Serpent*. New York: Vintage Books, 1989.

Pantel, Pauline Schmitt, ed. *A History of Women in the West: From Ancient Goddesses to Christian Saints*. Cambridge: The Belknap Press of Harvard University, 1992.

Peradotto, John and J.P, Sullivan. *Women in the Ancient World: The Arethusa Papers*. Albany: State University of New York Press, 1984.

Plaskow, Judith. *Standing Again at Sinai*. San Francisco: Harper Collins, 1990.

Plevnik, Joseph. "The Eyewitnesses of the Risen Jesus in Luke 24." *The Catholic Biblical Quarterly* 49 (January 1987):90–103.

Pomeroy, Sarah B. *Goddesses, Whores, Wives, and Slaves: Women in Classical Antiquity*. New York: Schocken Books, 1975.

Qeull, Gottfried. *"kurios," Theological Dictionary of the New Testament*. ed. by Gerhard Kittel. 10 vols. Grand Rapids, Michigan: Wm. B. Eerdmans Publishing Company, 1982. 3:1058–81.

Rahmani, L. Y. "Ancient Jerusalem's Funerary Customs and Tombs—Part One," *Biblical Archeologist* 44 (Summer 1981):171–77.

Reicke, Bo. *The New Testament Era: The World of the Bible from 500 B.C. to A.D. 100*. Philadelphia: Fortress Press, 1981.

Riches, John. *The World of Jesus: First-Century Judaism in Crisis*. New York: Cambridge University Press, 1990.

Robinson, Stephen E. "The Setting of the Gospels," in *Studies in Scripture: Volume Five, The Gospel*. Salt Lake City: Deseret Book Co., 1986. pp. 10–37.

Saldarini, Anthony J. "Pharisees," *The Anchor Bible Dictionary* ed.

David Noel Freeman, 6 Vols. New York: Doubleday, 1992. 5:289–303.

Sanders, E. P. *Jewish Law from Jesus to the Mishnah: Five Studies.* Philadelphia: Fortress Press, 1990.

Sanders, E. P. *Judaism: Practice & Belief, 63 BCE—66 CE.* Philadelphia: Trinity Press International, 1992.

Schaberg, Jane. *The Illegitimacy of Jesus: A Feminist Theological Interpretation of the Infancy Narratives.* San Francisco: Harper & Row, Publishers, 1987.

Schaber, Jane. "How Mary Magdalene Became A Whore," *Bible Review* 8 (October 1992):30–37.

Schrage, Wolfgang. "*Synagoge*," *Theological Dictionary of the New Testament.* ed. Gerhard Kittel. 10 vols. Grand Rapids, Michigan: Wm. B. Eerdmans Publishing Company, 1982. 7:830–33.

Schrenk, Gottlob. "*Ekdikeo*," *Theological Dictionary of the New Testament.* ed. by Gerhard Kittel. 10 vols. Grand Rapids, Michigan: Wm. B. Eerdmans Publishing Company, 1982. 2:442–46.

Segal, Alen F. *Rebecca's Children: Judaism and Christianity in the Roman World.* Cambridge: Harvard University Press, 1986.

Segal, Peretz. "The Penalty of the Warning Inscription from the Temple of Jerusalem," *Israel Exploration Journal* 39 (1989): 79–84.

Shelton, Jo-Ann. *As the Romans Did: A Source Book in Roman Social History.* New York: Oxford University Press, 1988.

Smith, Morton. "The Dead Sea Sect in Relation to Ancient Judaism," *New Testament Studies* 7 (1960–61): 347–60.

Spencer, Aida Besancon. *Beyond the Curse.* Peabody, Massachusetts: Hendrickson Publishers, 1985.

Stagg, Evelyn & Frank. *Woman in the World of Jesus.* Philadelphia: The Westminster Press, 1978.

Strack, Hermann L. *Introduction to the Talmud and Midrash.* Atheneum, New York: A Temple Book, 1976.

Strange, James F. and Hershel Shanks, "Has the House Where Jesus Stayed in Capernaum Been Found?" *Biblical Archaeology Review* 8 (November/December 1982):26–37.

Strange, James F. and Herschel Shanks, "Synagogue Where Jesus Preached found at Capernaum," *Biblical Archaeology Review.* 9 (November/December 1983):24–31.

Talmage, James E. *Jesus the Christ*. Salt Lake City: Deseret Book Co., 1970.

Tannehil, Robert C. *The Narrative Unity of Luke-Acts: A Literary Interpretation*. Volume 1. Philadelphia: Fortress Press, 1986.

Tarn, W. W. and G. T. Griffith. *Hellenistic Civilization*. London: Arnold, 1952.

Tetlow, Elisabeth M. *Women and Ministry in the New Testament*. New York: Paulist Press, 1980.

Tubb, Jonathan N. *Eyewitness Guides: Bible Lands*. London: Dorling Kindersley, 1991.

Veyne, Paul, ed. *A History of Private Life: From Pagan Rome to Byzantium*. Cambridge: Harvard University Press, 1987.

Veyne, Paul. *Bread and Circuses: Historical Sociology and Political Pluralism*. New York: Allen Lane The Penguin Press, 1990.

Wall, Robert W. "Divorce," *The Anchor Bible Dictionary*. ed. David Noel Freedman. 6 vols. New York: Doubleday, 1992. 2:217–19.

Wegner, Judith Romney. *Chattel or Person: The Status of Women in the Mishnah*. New York: Oxford University Press, 1988.

Wenham, Gordon J. "Betulah: A Girl of Marriageable Age," *Vetus Testamentum* 22 (July 1972):326–48.

Wilcox, Max. "Talitha Cumi," *The Anchor Bible Dictionary*. ed. David Noel Freedman. 6 vols. New York: Doubleday, 1992. 6:310.

Wilson, S.G. *Luke and the Law*. New York: Cambridge University Press, 1983.

Witherington, Ben, III. "Anti-Feminist Tendencies of the 'Western' Text in Acts." *Journal of Biblical Literature* 103 (1984) 1:82–84.

Witherington, Ben, III. *Women in the Ministry of Jesus*. Cambridge: Cambridge University Press, 1984.

Whittaker, Molly. *Jew & Christians: Graeco-Roman Views*. New York: Cambridge University Press, 1984.

Index